How to Write Essays and Dissertations

A GUIDE FOR ENGLISH LITERATURE STUDENTS

Second edition

NIGEL FABB AND ALAN DURANT

PEARSON

Longman

Harlow, England • London • New York • Boston • San Francisco • Toronto
Sydney • Tokyo • Singapore • Hong Kong • Seoul • Taipei • New Delhi
Cape Town • Madrid • Mexico City • Amsterdam • Munich • Paris • Milan

PEARSON EDUCATION LIMITED

Edinburgh Gate
Harlow CM20 2JE
United Kingdom
Tel: +44 (0)1279 623623
Fax: +44 (0)1279 431059
Website: www.pearsoned.co.uk

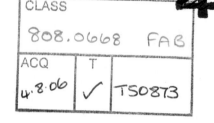

First edition published in 1993
Second edition published in 2005

© Pearson Education Limited 1993, 2005

The rights of Nigel Fabb and Alan Durant to be identified
as authors of this work have been asserted by them in
accordance with the Copyright, Designs and Patents Act 1988.

ISBN 0 582 78455 7

British Library Cataloguing in Publication Data
A CIP catalogue record for this book can be obtained from the British Library

Library of Congress Cataloging in Publication Data
Fabb, Nigel.
    How to write essays and dissertations : a guide for English literature students / Nigel
Fabb and Alan Durant.—2nd ed.
        p. cm.
    Includes bibliographical references and index.
        ISBN 0–582–78455–7 (pbk.)
        1. Criticism—Authorship—Handbooks, manuals, etc.   2. Literature—History and
criticism—Theory, etc.—Handbooks, manuals, etc.   3. Dissertations,
Academic—Authorship—Handbooks, manuals, etc.   4. English
language—Rhetoric—Handbooks, manuals, etc.   5. Essay—Authorship—Handbooks,
manuals, etc.   6. Academic writing—Handbooks, manuals, etc.   I. Durant, Alan.
II. Title.

PE1479.C7F33 2005
808'.0668—dc22

                                                                              2004060175

10 9 8 7 6 5 4 3 2 1
09 08 07 06 05

Set in 10.5/13pt Bembo by 35
Printed by Malaysia

The Publishers' policy is to use paper manufactured from sustainable forests.

Table of contents

If you are studying literature – whether at school, college or university – you will have to write essays. Those essays may take the form of exam answers, coursework projects or in some cases a longer dissertation, but they all have something in common. Each is meant to be difficult. If you don't find writing your essays difficult then something is wrong, since your teachers have set those essays largely because they expect you to learn from confronting difficulty. This book should help you to identify the difficulties presented by essay-writing and to work productively with them.

Being a good writer of an essay on literature means being a good reader, one who is able to make discoveries about a literary text. It also means being able to organise your time efficiently, so you can make the best use of the inevitably limited time you have available. Beyond these two skills, however, you also need to have a set of more specialised strategies for how to write; it is these strategies that this book should help you develop.

But why work on strategies that need to be learned and practised, rather than relying on your own individual creativity? After all, literary studies as a discipline has always been strongly committed to subjectivity and individuality; and an idiosyncratic essay may deserve to be rewarded far more than one which is clear and competent but lacks distinctive flair. (Many writers have discussed how the aims and methods of literary studies reflect values that vary between different places and times; and we ourselves have done so in other books which complement this one, including the practical guide Montgomery, Durant, Fabb, Furniss and Mills, *Ways of Reading: Advanced reading skills for students of English literature*.) It is an understandable reservation to be reluctant to nail down your interest in reading with rules for writing; but there is a reason to work on essay-writing strategies nevertheless: that even the most individual work – or perhaps especially the most individual work – builds on and refers to established conventions; you need to understand what those established conventions are if you are to work with (or against) them without being dominated or marginalised by them.

How to Write Essays and Dissertations: A Guide for English Literature Students is intended to be enabling rather than prescriptive. We recognise that it would be impossible to predict all the possible ways a good essay could be put together, and that prescriptive rules for writing risk inhibiting originality, stifling imaginative involvement in literature, cramping your style and turning literary study into a production line of variations on the same basic model. So instead of trying to tell you what to do, we offer ideas, models and suggestions to be used only where you judge them to be preferable to what you have done in the past or tend to do at present. Practical advice of this kind, and your reading of the examples we discuss, should enable you to benefit from norms and conventional devices without crushing your individual writing talents. Throughout, we emphasise how you might adapt our suggestions for your own purposes.

In the fifteen units which follow, we work through the process of writing an essay or dissertation step by step. For each essential task, from grasping the point of a question or formulating your own topic through to handing in a completed piece of work, we offer guidelines based on our experience as teachers and examiners and reflect on the assumptions and difficulties of particular techniques we introduce. We also give detailed commentary on extracts we have chosen to illustrate strengths and weaknesses of different ways of tackling each aspect of essay writing.

The examples we use to illustrate essay-writing strategies – both effective strategies and less effective ones – are taken from a range of levels of work: school 'A' Level essays, undergraduate coursework essays, projects and examination scripts. Occasionally we have also taken examples from postgraduate work to illustrate a particular point. Some of the writers whose work we discuss are native speakers of English; others are not (they are so-called 'non-native speakers'). The wide range of these sources reflects our view that many of the same basic problems are faced in writing literary essays at each level. Much of what we say should therefore be relevant whether you are preparing to write a short exam essay or doing postgraduate research. And although our examples are taken from courses and student research in English Literature, most of what we say is applicable to writing essays on literature in other languages, as well as to courses in cultural studies, media studies, art history and other humanities fields. The conventions and strategies we outline apply in all courses where essays of literary or cultural analysis are written in English.

Many of the essays we quote from, it should be remembered, are unfinished; and some examples have been taken from first drafts. Numerous errors remain in these extracts, both in those written by native speakers and in those written by non-native speakers. This is often exactly why the extracts are useful for our purposes. For reasons of space and continuity, however, we only comment on those features in any extract that are relevant to the particular topic under discussion. We are not recommending that you should imitate other features of the extracts simply because we have not discussed them.

Our wish in writing the first edition of this book, over ten years ago, was to address two difficulties we commonly met with in the different groups of students we were teaching. One difficulty was the range of reactions, from frustration through to depression, experienced by many students of literature when contemplating a blank page or an essay deadline. The other was the widespread underachievement of students who read and discuss literary works in interesting and original ways in class, but whose written work made little impression on examiners not personally acquainted with the writer. Ten years on, neither problem is any less common, and in this second edition we continue to address these same basic difficulties. But we have also tried to incorporate lessons from the new ways in which the same underlying, general difficulties are experienced by students now. So as well as updating the book generally, we have taken this opportunity to consider fresh essay-writing challenges presented by changing forms of assessment, use of word-processing as the principal means of writing and editing, and extensive use of internet materials.

INTRODUCTION

THE IMPORTANCE OF WRITING IN LITERARY STUDIES

A lot of the interest in studying literature comes from reading books. So does a lot of the pleasure. It seems reasonable, therefore, to think of a literature course as mainly a process of reading (and learning about) a series of prescribed or recommended works; in doing this as part of a structured programme of study, you develop specialised kinds of understanding and ability to investigate writing, and in this way you become proficient in the discipline.

This view of literary studies requires some qualification, however. It is true that the 'input' of your course consists largely of what you *read* and how you read it. But the assessed 'output' almost always consists of *writing*. Sometimes that writing takes the form of short written answers to prescribed questions (as it does in exams); sometimes it consists of extended coursework essays or dissertations. It is these written pieces, rather than your work in class or participation in seminar discussion, that form the main basis – in many cases the only basis – of the grades you are awarded.

Given such an emphasis on writing as the principal means of assessment in literary studies, the possibility arises that you might be able to succeed *primarily* on the basis of essay-writing skills, rather than on the strength of insights arrived at during reading. Such a view would be misguided. But it does capture an important point: that careful and sensitive reading counts for little in a course in literary studies unless it is linked to skills in constructing relevant

1

arguments on the written page. Your success in reading – at least in the sense of gaining recognition in your course for the interest and value of your insights – will remain invisible unless you also know how to write.

That is why this book investigates writing skills and the study skills that support essay-writing: in effect, how you can embody observations you make about literary texts in appropriate written form. To help you develop or strengthen such skills, we propose to work step by step through the major processes involved in writing in literary studies:

- interpreting a prescribed question, or thinking of your own title or topic;
- anticipating what markers will look for in your essay;
- working out your basic ideas;
- making a first sketch or outline;
- using reference sources to extend your ideas with appropriate information;
- developing your argument coherently, from its introduction through to its conclusion;
- monitoring aspects of composition, such as grammar, spelling, cohesion and punctuation;
- submitting your finished work in an accepted academic format.

In the course of the book we will make concrete suggestions about each of these aspects of essay-writing. Together, these suggestions should help you break down the sometimes confusing overall experience of writing an essay into a series of distinct steps or stages, each of which you can analyse and learn to control.

FOUR BASIC PRINCIPLES

Before moving on to practical concerns, we begin with four basic claims about writing.

A. Writing means construction.
B. Writing involves a continuous process of re-construction.

C. Writing is a way of thinking.

D. Writing is different from talking.

Gaining a grasp of each of these claims can help overcome the most pervasive misunderstandings students have about what they are being asked to do. After discussing each claim in general terms, we put them together in order to suggest some specific ways you can use this book to improve your study and writing skills.

A. Writing means construction

In this book we do not treat writing as an activity of immediate self-expression, in which you pour out ideas spontaneously and inspirationally. Instead, we treat writing as a process of composition: a craft of making or building something.

Books are *read many times but are written only once*. Almost the opposite is the case with essays written for literature courses: essays have to be written (in the sense of modified, altered or drafted) many times; but then they are probably only read by your reader once.

A large part of what you need to learn is accordingly how to take control of and steer the repeated stages of writing and rewriting that reshape your initial thoughts into a coherent, sustained argument that will have a clear and immediate impact. Many of the difficulties people encounter in writing essays arise because of the need to control a number of different aspects of organisation at the same time. You need to control:

- *the argument*: so that the essay will be coherent at a conceptual level;
- *the information structure*: to avoid presenting, as if they were new, facts or views likely to be well-known to and presupposed by your reader;
- *the discourse structure*: so that your essay builds up, and has shape and development;
- *the style*: so that the essay speaks in a voice you are comfortable with and which meets the expectations of your course;
- *the punctuation and grammar*: so that the essay can be read easily and unambiguously;

- *the presentation*: so that the essay can be read clearly in terms of layout, handwriting and typeface.

B. Writing involves a constant process of re-construction

There are some writers who gestate an idea mentally for a long time, then write it down perfectly formed. But such writers are a minority. Most writing – whether it takes the form of poetry, committee reports, memos and minutes of meetings, or literary essays – passes through successive revisions. It is repeatedly modified in the light of what a given expression of ideas looks like on the page. Most people find it easier to reflect on their thoughts once they are on the page, rather than trying to shape what will be a piece of writing while it remains a complex idea in their head.

The approach to writing we will encourage challenges the common belief (which you may still hear from some teachers and research supervisors) that you should start by doing all your reading and only then begin writing. On the contrary, we think you should do at least some writing before you read. Writing helps you understand what it is you will need from the books you read; the notes you take will be much more focused as a result. Writing also points you towards other books – and particular facts and arguments in them – that you will need to read but hadn't previously thought of. Abstract intentions, and theoretical knowledge of what good writing may be like, need to take a back seat here to the practical approach of 'try it on the page, see what it looks like, and then decide whether to keep it or how to change it'.

C. Writing is a way of thinking

Writing is a tool. Like diagrams, maps or numerical calculations, it is a resource to think with. Writing helps you organise and manipulate ideas into sequences or systems that cannot easily be held simultaneously in your mind. Importantly, it is also a tool you carry with you beyond literary studies: a so-called 'transferable skill'. Studying literature is widely believed to provide training in thinking, and this book should help you make the writing process central to that training.

If you view writing as a means of thinking, rather than a way of telling someone something, then irrespective of who reads your essays they are vehicles for developing solutions to intellectual problems you set yourself. The process of writing in itself offers ways of working through questions in a more reflective and considered form than is possible in most spoken contexts of conversation or discussion. Seen in this way, writing an essay can provide a degree of satisfaction, and increased self-confidence, ultimately as valuable as the marks with which it is rewarded.

D. Writing is different from talking

When you talk to someone, your hearer can let you know whether or not they understand what you are saying. Your hearer can stop you and ask you to explain or clarify something. But your *reader* cannot ask for clarification in the same way, and you cannot ask your reader whether she or he has understood. You therefore need to provide everything essential for understanding in the written text itself; you can't rephrase any parts that didn't get across first time. This is one reason why writing is typically more formal and bound by more explicit rules than speaking.

However, 'providing everything essential' brings its own problems. If you provide too much background information, your reader will become bored and lose attention. So you need constantly to make decisions, as precisely as possible, about how much information your reader will need. You should not create the appearance of going over too much old ground.

Your essay unfolds over the period of time a reader takes to read it; so your choices about information are not only a matter of more-or-less. There also needs to be clear direction and development in what you write. Your essay should lead towards a clearly-signalled goal, rather than merely listing or presenting material whose relevance to your discussion hasn't been explicitly established. When in doubt, there is a useful check you can carry out on yourself: imagine yourself as a reader of your work who keeps asking: why is she/he telling me this?

PRACTICE AND EXPERIMENTATION

Because writing is different from speech, it is possible to think of writing as a sort of 'foreign language', in that most people use the 'language' of written English with less fluency than they use the 'language' of spoken English. Improving your writing is like improving your use of a foreign language: practice helps.

Practice in essay-writing involves first putting boundaries round a writing task. For example, set a time limit of 40 minutes, and try to write a complete essay in this time (using an old exam question, perhaps); doing this successfully involves learning how to plan and time your work, and is of course useful in examinations. You should judge your success *given the time permitted.*

Alternatively, practice can mean taking special care over one small section of work. Take a fairly self-contained page or short section or paragraph from an essay and keep rewriting it, analysing the results of successive revisions.

Or try carrying out different parts of a task, in isolation from the overall process of writing an essay. For instance:

- work out what a question is asking you, without trying to answer it;
- make a list of paragraph headings for essays you don't ever intend to write in full.

Learn from your practice, and keep notes of what you have learned. Next time you can avoid repeating mistakes by applying to a new writing task the general strategies you've already used successfully on at least one previous occasion.

PREPARING FOR WORK

Practice is all very well, but you can only practise effectively if you set yourself up to work effectively, and everyone works differently. Some kinds of improvement in your work may follow simply from thinking about how best *you* work and trying to make suitable practical arrangements.

Look for ways of making time for yourself to work, and a place where you can work productively. Home may be too full of distractions, and the boundary between work and other activities may be too thin there, so you may need to define somewhere else as your working place. If your working space is also your bedroom, then you may be in danger of not building a clear enough barrier between the stresses of your work and your need to sleep. If the library isn't quiet, look for an empty room somewhere else, and work there. Exploit gaps; take something to read on the bus or while waiting in a queue. Keep a pen on you and some paper so that you can record good ideas whenever you have them.

These ideas as regards techniques follow from taking a long view of what you are doing, rather than expecting instant outcomes. Accept that you may spend a day at your computer while writing nothing of value, and that such unproductive periods are inevitable. Expect things to go wrong and plan for them; your printer breaks, or the mail is unreliable, or the library is shut. Vary the tasks you do during the day, so that tasks that seem boring or unpleasant are balanced out by easier and more enjoyable tasks. Be tough with yourself, however, about the difference between productive work and other displacement activities that can be ways of pretending to work (e.g. putting extensive effort into the visual layout of your document). Remember that it always takes longer to finish something (e.g. by getting your bibliography right, or proof-reading or printing) than you anticipate, and allow time for such tasks. Understand the deadlines set for you, and what happens if you fail to meet them. Finally keep in mind that, although each aspect of the writing process is something to think about and work on, you are almost always judged on what you produce, not on how you produced it.

EXERCISE

In the section 'Practice and experimentation' above, we illustrated the value of practising writing by suggesting some possible
tasks you could set yourself. Read this section again. Choose
two tasks we propose there that make contrasting demands on
your writing (e.g. one involves 'speed writing' a whole essay to a
specified time limit; another involves intensive editing of a short
passage). When you have finished the two suggested tasks, make
a list of the main difficulties you encountered with each, and
compare the two lists. Use the contents page and index of this
book to see where the different problem areas identified in your
lists are discussed.

Unit 2

WRITING ON A PRESCRIBED TOPIC

Much of the attraction of literary studies arises because the field encourages you to express individual thoughts and opinions. But when you answer set essay questions, for example in exams or when a specific coursework topic is prescribed, the problem you are expected to address has already been identified for you. The pre-scribed question outlines a problem and usually also points you in a direction for solving it. In this unit we describe the main kinds of prescribed question set in literary studies and what they ask you to do. We also offer some exam-question and exam-room strategies that should help you make the most of insights from your reading, even when you do not have much time to present them.

WHAT ESSAY QUESTIONS ASK YOU TO DO

The typical essay in literary studies requires you to be both know-ledgeable and original. The knowledge you demonstrate is of the contents of a book, the conventions of a literary-critical approach, the historical circumstances of a writer, and/or the views of critics. Your originality is shown by discovering and reporting something not previously known, or by constructing a new argument from ideas and information you have taken from somewhere else. The two qualities are linked: your originality emerges from, and refers back to, what you know; in academic writing your ideas and discoveries are always part of a network made up of the ideas and discoveries of others. The integration of your own work with other people's work is achieved by writing a particular kind of essay, an essay which constructs an argument in four stages:

- identify a problem or issue in a given area;
- establish competing points of view associated with the issue identified;
- present evidence in support of and against various positions which might be taken up with regard to that issue;
- reach a conclusion consistent with the evidence and arguments you have presented.

TYPES OF PRESCRIBED QUESTION

We now outline the main tasks that coursework and exam questions in literary studies ask you to undertake. Remember, though, that a question might ask you to do more than one thing, and you may in any case decide that a comparison (between texts, periods, styles, etc.) would be useful in constructing a debate even where the question only explicitly requires you to write about a single case.

Debate or evaluation

This type of question may include the words 'comment on', or 'discuss', or 'assess', or 'justify'. Or it may ask, 'Do you agree with the assertion that . . .'. Often this kind of question includes a sentence in quotation marks which you are expected to comment on, with the quotation either given a source or alternatively made up by the examiners. Sometimes the question will include the words 'to what extent' or 'in what ways does . . .'. These words indicate an expectation that you will demonstrate partial agreement and partial disagreement with the question. Debate means reasoned presentation of arguments for and against a proposition, with a conclusion – no matter how qualified or tentative – reached at the end.

Q: To what extent should Heaney's poetry be described and assessed in terms drawn from his own critical essays?

Q: 'Derrida's approach to reading encourages only scepticism about the possibility of meaning in literature.' Discuss.

Q: 'Psychoanalytic criticism can merge with other kinds of reading without supplanting them: it can underpin without undermining.' Have you found this to be so?

Q: Can there be a 'science of the text'?

You should generally find that the answer is not at one end or the other of the available continuum or spectrum, but somewhere in the middle. And the answer is never just a long version of 'yes' or 'no', even if the question is phrased in a directly interrogative way. Passionate disagreement (or agreement) with questions is usually inappropriate: the question doesn't adequately present any-one's genuine opinion, but offers a constructed or quoted opinion which is being used to provoke and focus a reaction. The examiners are asking you to show that you have a view and can justify it, whatever it is.

Analysis, exploration and classification

This type of question may include the words 'analyse', or 'in what ways does . . .', or 'explore', or 'differentiate', or 'classify', or 'describe the types of'. Such questions test your knowledge of a text and expect you to display your accurate knowledge of technical terms, literary genres, kinds of poetic strategy, kinds of narrative feature.

Q: In what ways can Wendy Cope's poetry be regarded as subversive?

Don't just answer this question with a list. Discuss the relationship between the different ways, and be as explicit as you can about connections between them.

Comparison

This type of question may include the words 'compare' and 'contrast'. If you are able to choose your own texts to compare or contrast, the best choice will be two texts which differ in some clear and interesting way but are similar in other ways; this enables you to focus on the significance of the clear difference.

> Q: Differentiate the dramaturgic procedures used in *two or more* plays you have studied during the course.

As you identify and compare whichever dramaturgic processes you identify, try to build up a system of classification, explaining the basis for the distinctions you are making.

Exemplification or description

This type of question may ask you to 'illustrate', or 'give examples of', or 'outline', or 'sketch', or 'summarise', perhaps telling you which texts or how many texts to use. Here you are expected to provide short quotations from a text or briefly summarise one; in such cases 'short' and 'brief' are important considerations, particularly in an exam. You will be rewarded less for what you can remember of a text or find in it than for the sense you can make of it, and the way you use that understanding in your essay.

> Q: Consider some of the expressive purposes of the rendition of places in Henry James's work.
>
> Q: Write a short essay on humour in Joseph Heller's *Catch-22*.

In the second of these questions, it is necessary to make clear your own interpretation of what 'write' means. Roughly, you can take it as synonymous with 'describe and discuss'. The difficulty here is that, since relatively little essay structure is signalled by the question itself, you will need in your first paragraph to make clear to your examiner what shape you are imposing on your discussion.

So in summary this is what you are asked to do in responding to set essay questions.

- You are to discuss a proposition, offering and evaluating arguments with appropriate illustration on different sides.
- The arguments should lead towards a conclusion, which (i) follows the arguments you have offered, and (ii) matches the balance for and against different possibilities that you argued for in your essay.

EXAM QUESTIONS

We now turn from the demands of essay questions in general to some specific features of how questions are typically structured in exams. Then we move on to outline some more general exam-room strategies that may be helpful when you are faced with a whole paper made up of such questions.

Most exam questions are constructed to explore the following aspects of your work.

- Exam questions seek to find out whether you can remember what you were taught in class (which in turn is partly a test of whether you attended), and to check whether you have read the set texts. In general, you will do better if you can show not only that you remember what was in the classes but also that you can adapt that material to new circumstances.
- Exam questions test your ability to think abstractly, and try to discover how far you can apply what you have learned in class to a problem that you have not previously been asked to consider.

> Q: 'In natural objects we feel ourselves, or think of
>   ourselves, only by likenesses – among men too
>   often by differences' (Coleridge). In the light of this
>   statement consider the presentation of the relation-
>   ship between the self and the world in the work of
>   any *one* writer of the period.

Here the quote from Coleridge picks out a general problem. The essay does not ask you to write about Coleridge. It may well be that you can demonstrate your ability to deal with the problem better if you write about some other author, rather than keeping close to the quotation you are given. Nevertheless, the attribution to Coleridge may still guide you: perhaps this problem is particularly well addressed by writing about an author from the same period as Coleridge.

• Exam questions test your ability to improvise and think creatively in a stressful and time-limited situation (some people,
  though they are rare, do their best work in this hothouse situation). The requirement to think without specific preparation is
  sometimes reflected in questions that are deliberately difficult.
  For example a question may exploit word-play to create extra
  difficulty:

> Q: Is contemporary drama more concerned with the
>   absence of families or with absent families?

With such questions, one of your tasks is to unpack the word-play. You have to make clear the distinctions you are drawing from the formulation of the question. You can usefully begin by saying that this is what you are doing, and then continue to work with the given definitions throughout the essay, relating the different definitions back to one another in the conclusion.

In the exam room

Here are some general tips.

- *Open with an introduction*: although it may seem surprising to say so, we believe that the beginning of an essay often has the most influence on its mark; your marker starts to decide after the first couple of sentences how much potential the essay has, in the form you are outlining for it, and so how good it is likely to be. So take special care: write an introductory paragraph, but don't use it as a way to put off answering the question. Instead use the first paragraph to translate the question into your own words. Don't translate 'word for word', however: reformulating and reorganising the question forces you to understand it and shows your examiner that you do. Translate technical words in the question into ordinary language wherever possible.
- *Provide a conclusion*: the question may not directly ask for a conclusion, but you should provide one anyway. Remember that, alongside the first sentence, it will be the final sentence that is most likely to influence your mark.
- *Give examples*: the question may not tell you to give examples, but you should; and you should show how those examples relate to the main substance of your answer.
- *Comment on what you are doing*: where a question seems broad or general, explain how you are interpreting it in order to make it more manageable. But don't talk about yourself or comment on the fact that you are doing an exam unless you are explicitly asked to. Your exam answer is not a letter you are writing to the examiner.
- *Organise your time*: give equal time to answers that can gain equivalent marks. Put most time into kinds of writing that stand to gain most marks, and try not to spend too much time on unrewarding work (e.g. don't copy out sections of text, don't use correction fluid to remove errors, don't copy out the question, don't retell the story). Make sure you answer all the questions you are asked to answer, even if your answer in some cases is sketchy.

Planning your answer to an exam question

Almost every exam question asks you to do several distinct things. Begin by jotting down what you think they are, plus any related thoughts this process triggers off. This stage resembles planning an essay outline (see Unit 7), and may provide you with your necessary paragraph headings (particularly since an exam essay allows space for only a few paragraphs). The question is now in simpler units which you can address in turn. These might include:

- problems in the formulation of the question – words which need definition or explanation, for example;
- established views on the issue raised by the question, which you are likely to have learned about in class or by your own reading;
- examples you can use to illustrate specific points (list the points that each example illustrates);
- crucial technical terms you need to introduce (e.g. an appropriate vocabulary for describing the rhyme scheme of a poem);
- historical context that needs to be introduced in order to answer a question about a writer from an earlier period.

Take note of how boundaries to a question are suggested by the way it is formulated, such as 'with reference to at least two works', or 'with reference to works by at least two authors', or 'choose *two* plays'. Divide up the time available for the question; this will mean that your answer, though short, is still properly proportioned.

EXERCISE

Select one exam question we have included in this chapter. Make a series of paragraph or section headings that you could use in a one-hour exam answer to it. You do not need to know much about the subject matter to draw up the headings; you only need to be able to identify what you would *need* to know. Bear in mind not only the length but also the proportion of your answer, and make sure that each relevant issue in the question is addressed.

DEVISING YOUR OWN TOPIC

When you answer a set question it is essential to think about exactly what kind of question you are answering and approach the topic accordingly (Unit 2). But if you have a free choice of topic you are setting your own question and need to work out how to approach it for yourself. In this unit, we work through two related processes: (i) narrowing down the topic, and (ii) imposing a structure on your treatment of that topic. We end by showing how suitably chosen combinations of essay focus and mode of argument create coherent overall projects.

SOME QUESTIONS TO ASK YOURSELF

What is the question I want to answer?

Having an idea of a general area of interest is often the starting point for an essay: a wish to write on 'something around X' (where X is most commonly an author, a work, a literary theme or a period). Right from the start, however, it is important to sharpen this sense of an area of interest by formulating it in terms of questions rather than broad, and inevitably vague, descriptive phrases.

> If you start from an area of interest which is 'Irony in Jane Austen's novel *Emma*', try to work out some questions to ask, such as, 'Do any of the characters in *Emma* deliberately

> use irony?'; 'Which characters use irony? Which don't?';
> 'Is there a distinction between the way men use irony and
> women use irony in *Emma*?', etc.

Collecting all the questions you can think of won't give you a
coherent focus for your essay, however. Once you have a cluster of
questions, you need to encapsulate as many as you can in a single
basic question, like this:

> Which types of characters in *Emma* use irony and why?

This reformulated question can now be researched and written
about in a way that the original broadly defined area couldn't be.

What can I expect by way of an answer?

Having identified a main question, you will find it helpful to make
as full a list as possible of the kinds of answer that are possible in
principle; you can then at least consider candidates that your essay
may in due course reject.

> The question 'Which types of character in *Emma* use irony
> and why?' is actually two questions. Answering the first part
> involves classifying characters into types; so it is useful to
> think of all types which might be relevant in answering the
> question – male versus female, old versus young, poor versus
> rich, as many types as you can think of. Some contrasts may
> immediately appear irrelevant, but it is necessary to consider
> them briefly, if only to see why you are ruling them out.
> Answering the second part, 'why?' depends on your answer
> to the first part. But it is useful anyway to speculate about
> possible findings: what kinds of things could count as
> explanations. The characters who use irony might be similar

in type to Austen herself (in class, gender, age); or they might be characters who function as heroes and heroines in the novels. Each of these answers raises further questions. This is exactly how you build your essay, as a sequence of questions which give rise to answers that prompt new questions.

What methods will help me find an answer?

Your essay needs to provide evidence or reasons for your point of view. Constantly ask, 'what have I noticed in the text or in background materials about the context that makes me think this?' Even if your reasoning seems self-evident to you, it won't to other people; they will come at the issue from a slightly (or perhaps a very) different point of view.

How can you show your reader that you have made an exhaustive survey of the characters in *Emma* and whether or not they use irony? Drawing up a list of all speaking characters is an obvious start (perhaps with a note of which pages they speak on and who they speak to). Putting all this information into a table might then be a good way to gather data together so that you can see clearly if there are any relevant generalisations to be made. You can put the table into your essay if the information turns out to be significant; or the table might just function as a way of leading you on to a different, better way of investigating the same question.

Will my chosen field expand indefinitely?

Bear in mind that background material can expand infinitely; it needs to be closed off somewhere, or given a boundary, to prevent you becoming submerged in a project that can't be completed. Take care not to include everything you are interested in, for the sole reason of bringing it in somewhere.

> Avoid the 'Jane Austen, gender, class, early nineteenth-century society and the development of the novel' type of project; such a project includes everything but inevitably lacks a clear focus.

How does my topic relate to current work in the field?

It may be that the question you wish to ask is different from the sorts of discussion you have encountered in what you have read on the subject. If so, indicate that you know this, if possible with an explanation of how your approach differs. Or it may be that the question you are interested in has been discussed before, but that you want to develop it in a different way, or to extend it, or to disagree with one of its premises. Again, indicate this, as precisely as possible. Establishing how your work fits into debate in the area is an important aspect of essay-writing in literary studies. Generally speaking, you need to know and to be able to show how and why your work *matters*.

> For the *Emma* essay, you could look in a bibliography for links between 'irony', 'Austen' and 'characterisation'; and you could scan some collections of essays on Austen or *Emma* for possibly relevant material. Similarly you could look in books on irony, in order to see how closely your ideas resemble existing material, and what aspects are original.

Am I interested enough?

With exam questions, you have little choice about whether you are interested enough to keep yourself motivated until you've finished. But then you also have only a short period of time. Some pieces of work, on the other hand, require a lot of reading and study time. For these you are likely to produce better work if you choose questions that genuinely interest you, or connect with problems you are interested in outside your studies, rather than if you feel your work is being done to no purpose, or simply out of obligation.

Be wary, though, of topics in which you feel very deeply immersed personally. You should depend primarily on knowledge you learn as part of your academic work, and not from your personal life experiences. You should also avoid writing as 'a fan', and in general keep clear of a topic if you feel it will be difficult to stand back sufficiently from it to carry out the sorts of procedures we have discussed in this unit.

> If you have a general political interest in social class, this could support an investigation of class as it relates to characters' use of irony in *Emma*.

GIVING YOUR CHOSEN TOPIC A STRUCTURE

Having looked at different sorts of decision that need to be made in formulating a project, we can now generalise. A literature essay always has a **focus** for its subject matter (a question shaped out of an area of interest); it should also always have a particular **mode of argument**. Each of these aspects of an essay has predictable characteristics. Consider focus first.

Essay focus

Here are some typical kinds of **focus**.

(i) AUTHORS

'The life and works of John Steinbeck'; 'women Romantic poets'.

(ii) TEXTS

Coleridge's 'Kubla Khan'; Ralph Ellison's *Invisible Man*; selected poems by Christina Rossetti.

(iii) GENERIC GROUPINGS OF TEXTS

The sonnet; eighteenth-century pastoral poetry; kitchen-sink drama.

(iv) HISTORICAL ISSUES RELATING TO A TEXT OR GROUP OF TEXTS

The specifically nineteenth-century idea of beauty in the nineteenth-century novel; developments in the theatre immediately before the English Civil War; representations of industrial life in early twentieth-century novels.

(v) THEORETICAL ISSUES RELATING TO LITERARY STUDY

Comparison of post-structuralist approaches to the lyric poem; the mental processes involved in understanding a metaphor; manipulations of point-of-view in narrative.

Mode of argument

Here are some typical modes of argument. These allow you, in approaching the point of focus of your material, to create something new and interesting.

(a) REVALUE A REPUTATION (OR ASSESS RELATIVE ACHIEVEMENT)

An extended essay that argues that Carol Ann Duffy is a major English poet who has not been taken sufficiently seriously because she writes humorously.

(b) ANALYSE STYLE: COMMENT ON ASPECTS OF THE LANGUAGE OF A TEXT

An essay pointing out that Shakespeare's first sonnet ends with a comma in the first printed edition and arguing that this is because it is the first part of a larger poem including also the second sonnet.

(c) RELATE A TEXT TO THE HISTORICAL CIRCUMSTANCES WHICH PRODUCED IT, OR IN WHICH IT IS READ

An essay which looks at the relation between the spread of tourism in the countryside in eighteenth-century Britain and the development of a new style of 'countryside' poetry exemplified in Wordsworth and Coleridge's *Lyrical Ballads*, published near the end of that century.

(d) PLACE A TEXT IN A LITERARY OR AESTHETIC CONTEXT (E.G. IN A TRADITION, IN THE EMERGENCE OF A NEW FORM OR STYLE)

A dissertation arguing that Robert Louis Stevenson should be understood as an early example of twentieth-century Modernism rather than as a late example of nineteenth-century Realism.

(e) DESCRIBE OR INTERPRET (OR REINTERPRET) A TEXT

An essay which describes the narrative of Alasdair Gray's novel *Lanark* and interprets it as a symbolic representation of the state of late twentieth-century Scotland.

(f) TAKE SIDES IN AN ONGOING CRITICAL ARGUMENT BETWEEN DIFFERING VIEWPOINTS

A thesis which investigates the made-up words in James Joyce's *Finnegans Wake* which resemble slips of the tongue, compares literary-theoretical approaches with experimental psychological approaches, and concludes that the psychological approaches undermine the validity of the literary-theoretical approaches.

(g) EXEMPLIFY THEORIES, TERMS OR APPROACHES, OR USE A CLASSIFICATORY SYSTEM TO DESCRIBE A TEXT, USUALLY IN ORDER TO ASSESS HOW SUITABLE OR EFFECTIVE THE DESCRIPTIVE SYSTEM IS

An essay showing that the linguistic theory of Conversational Analysis can help us understand how characters in *The Glass Menagerie* by Tennessee Williams control each other through the ways they interact in speech.

Combining focus and mode of argument

Essay projects can be devised by combining a given essay focus with a particular mode of argument, though not all combinations are automatically as interesting as each other. Consider, as an example of a combination of a selected focus with one of the modes of argument outlined above, an essay with a focus on R.K. Narayan's *The*

Guide [focus (ii)], which argues that it is underrated and indicates why it should be viewed as a more significant achievement [mode of argument (a)]. Note that more than one focus can be adopted in any given essay, and different modes of argument can be combined. In our example, the evaluation of *The Guide* could involve a stylistic argument, so combining mode of argument (a) with mode of argument (b).

While a single essay may draw on more than one perspective, however, it is important to establish which is the primary or organising mode of argument and what is the primary focus around which the essay is based. Otherwise you risk obscuring the development of your essay by failing to signal clearly its overall direction. Many essays suffer from exactly this problem: they lack a sufficiently clear sense of what the main issues are. Other essays are damaged by what appears to be the opposite problem, but is actually a result of the same lack of structure: they read as if they are trying to solve two or more problems at once.

GIVING YOUR ESSAY A TITLE

There is no rush to find a title for your essay; you can decide it at any stage. Your title can lead the process of writing, as a source of questions and ideas. Or it can be chosen at the very end, encapsulating the main points of an argument you have already written.

As regards your title's form of words, there are typical formulae you can build on, especially the common form 'title colon sub-title':

The Text and the Reader: Construction of meaning in fiction by Umberto Eco *(title of a Master's thesis)*

Marx and Spenser: Elizabeth and the problem of Imperial Power *(draft title of a PhD thesis)*

The formula here is not just two points about the essay linked by a colon, but also requires a combination of two different styles: the main title is in a verbally adroit, catchy form or alternatively is in some way vague or enigmatic; the sub-title offers a gloss or explanatory paraphrase in more conventionally academic language.

Consider in this light one possible title for the Naryan topic used as an example above:

> Undervalued achievement: the contribution of R.K. Narayan's
> *The Guide* to the development of post-colonial fiction

This title illustrates both types of contrast. The phrase before the colon is enigmatic: it states a provocative combination of value and perceived injustice, but without referring to anything in particular. This contrasts with the phrase after the colon, which consists of more conventional literary critical terminology: author name; book title; literary genre ('fiction'). As regards topic, the phrase after the colon indicates what the essay is about, in that the author's name and the title of the work signal the essay's main focus, with the phrase 'the development of post-colonial fiction' providing necessary context. But even when you have read the sub-title, you have to go back to the main title, 'Undervalued achievement', to find what we have called the mode of argument: the point of view and sense of purpose that will drive the essay.

EXERCISE

Select a novel you have just read. Following procedures outlined in this unit, construct a brief summary of the main points you might include in each of the following types of argument about the book:

- stylistic
- contextual
- evaluation of conflicting critical arguments

Compare your three summaries.

WHAT MARKERS WANT

Sometimes it is said that to get good grades you have to keep a particular marker in mind as you write. Your essay is then like a letter to your marker. Some students even say they tailor their essays substantially to the preferences (or imagined prejudices) of that marker, who is usually also their course tutor. This strategy may be effective if you're in a small class. But it's unlikely to work if you're writing your essay in circumstances where there are many different people who might mark it, or where the essay will be double-marked. The strategy won't work either if you take a public exam; in that case you have absolutely no idea who will do the marking.

The belief that you should tailor work for a particular marker is largely misguided. This is less an ethical than a practical judgement. One reason not to shape your essay in this way, for instance, is that assessment schemes have become increasingly explicit, so individual tastes of any given marker are largely subordinate to stated **assessment criteria** within an overall marking scheme. Such assessment criteria are not there to provide you with a checklist of what to do. But where they exist, you can strengthen your essay-writing by working with them, and in this unit we show you how. At the end of the unit, we return to the issue of whether it might still be worth keeping someone specific in mind as you write.

ASSESSMENT CRITERIA

In some cases assessment criteria are formulated by an individual course tutor. Where this is so, you will find them in your course outline or in a class hand-out. Alternatively, the criteria may form part of more general institutional policies or regulations. In such cases, you need to look beyond your course materials. Information is typically available in such cases in your general programme hand-book, and/or on the website of your college or university. If you are taking a public examination, such as A Level or Scottish Higher, you can find such information on the website of the assessment board whose syllabus you are following (e.g. Edexcel or AQA (Assessment and Qualifications Alliance). Read such assessment criteria before you start writing; they can guide you towards decisions both on what to write about, and also on appropriate ways of illustrating and justifying whatever you do finally write.

Outline of assessment criteria

Drawing on a range of course and exam documents, we now describe the main assessment criteria you might expect to find in assessment schemes for literary studies.

Fluent expression of personal response
Sometimes the criterion of **personal response** is expressed in terms such as, 'produce fluent and convincing responses demonstrating close and detailed reading of texts', or 'articulate independent opinions and judgements'. You are rewarded for showing that you have engaged personally with the work(s) you are discussing, and have something to report back from your own reading experience.

Contextualising your personal response
This criterion places a value on stepping back from your own read-ing, putting it in a larger, literary and historical perspective. That larger perspective typically consists of three different but linked elements.

1. *Context*: this means both the historical circumstances in which the text was written – 'the relevance of the author's life and his/her other works' – and also any relevant connections or comparisons you see with other texts that may give the text extra significance: 'the significance of literary traditions, periods and movements in relation to texts studied'.

2. *Other readers' likely interpretations*: in providing a context for your reading, you are encouraged to show awareness that other readers may 'attribute different meanings and value to the same text without necessarily misunderstanding or misreading it'. Essays which show that their writers are aware of different possible readings can demonstrate that their writers are 'sensitive to the scope of their own and others' interpretations of texts', and reflect 'ability to appreciate and discuss varying opinions of literary works'.

3. *Assumptions that shape the writer's own interpretation*: such assumptions include cultural or religious beliefs that underpin your reading but will vary from reader to reader. Showing awareness of how such assumptions affect interpretation involves 'acknowledging that literary texts have a range of meanings and the significance of these is related to readers' knowledge, experience and ideas.'

Recognition of how 'form, structure and language' shape a text's meaning

Terms such as **form**, **structure** and **language** range in meaning from local effects such as rhyme schemes, patterns of metaphor, or shifts of point of view through to larger choices made by an author, including narrative style and genre. What is rewarded here, in general, is seeing meaning as an outcome of 'the power of words and their arrangement to signify and to inspire', not as something separate from, or somehow in parallel with, the text.

Use of appropriate literary-critical concepts and terminology

Using literary-critical terms appropriately is taken to show 'familiarity with established ways of talking and writing about texts'. Quite often this criterion is qualified by phrases such as 'with understanding and discrimination', in order to emphasise that marks are not given just for using technical vocabulary to achieve a professional-sounding style, but only where literary-critical concepts and terminology add something to an argument.

Key skills of organisation and presentation
Such skills are typically said to include 'clear and coherent organisation of relevant information, using specialist vocabulary when appropriate', plus use of textual evidence in the form of quotation, paraphrase or relevant narration of detail. Better grades are awarded to 'confident and fluent written expression in an appropriate style'. Statements of this criterion generally remind you that students will 'be assessed according to their ability to ensure text is legible, and spelling, grammar and punctuation are accurate, so that meaning is clear.'

Making sensible use of assessment criteria

You are writing your essay, not marking it; so how can you benefit from assessment criteria that are in the end guidelines for someone else? One route is to check how the assessment criteria apply in your particular case. Sometimes each criterion or heading is used in allocating a proportion of the available marks (e.g. 10% for essay style, 20% for familiarity with the text, etc.). In other marking schemes, the marker is directed towards sources of evidence to be drawn on in support of a single, overall judgement that will reflect how the various elements work together.

While it can be worth knowing how you will be marked, it is important not to become preoccupied by this. More important is to keep in mind the essential point that each assessment criterion describes what the writer is required to **demonstrate**, a word which emphasises that your qualities as a writer will be inferred from evidence in the essay itself. Your skills as a reader of literature are evaluated on the strength of features of your writing about literature, not treated as aspects of personality that you carry round with you.

To use assessment criteria constructively, therefore, you need to see them not as personal attributes but as features of writing. Use them, for example, to create prompt-questions in planning your essay.

- Is what I feel about this text likely to be how other people view it?
- Is there a historical reason why this aspect of the text is as it is?
- Where will I get evidence to support this point?

Later, as you revise and edit, you will find such prompts useful again. They help you check how far your essay has in fact covered the prescribed ground. Using assessment criteria to shape such self-questioning doesn't mean being limited by prescriptive rules; rather, it allows you to test your own developing ideas against an underlying, general project design.

LEARNING OUTCOMES

Documented assessment criteria often relate back to stated 'learning outcomes' for a whole programme of study. Such **learning outcomes** describe the sorts of knowledge and skill you are expected to have if you complete the programme successfully. In this way a programme's learning outcomes amount to a sort of assessment baseline or threshold standard: to pass the course you need to show you have reached a minimum standard in each specified area.

As with assessment criteria, you can find statements of learning outcomes in course outlines or on the course website. Like a set of boxes inside boxes, learning outcomes are often formulated in such a way that they, in turn, reflect more general learning outcomes for awards in other subjects offered by the same institution. Sometimes, an over-arching framework of learning outcomes will exist for a given subject; where this is the case, a statement of those outcomes will be found on the website of the relevant regulatory body (e.g. in Britain, the Qualifications and Curriculum Authority [QCA] or the Quality Assurance Agency for Higher Education [QAA]), for which they act as a discipline-specific 'benchmark'.

Example of learning outcomes

Here is a typical statement of programme learning outcomes for an English literature BA degree course.

A. KNOWLEDGE AND UNDERSTANDING

On completion of this programme the successful student will have an appropriate range of knowledge and understanding of:

1. Literature from different periods

2. The role of literary criticism in shaping literary interpretation and value

3. The distinctive nature of texts written in the principal literary genres

4. Linguistic, literary, cultural and socio-historical contexts in which literature is written and read

5. The variety of critical and theoretical approaches to literary study

6. How literature produces and reflects cultural change and difference.

B. COGNITIVE (THINKING) SKILLS

On completion of the programme the successful student will have a range of specialised skills:

1. Deploy skills in the close reading and analysis of texts

2. Articulate knowledge and understanding of texts, concepts and theories relating to English studies at an abstract level

3. Articulate how different social and cultural contexts affect the nature of language and meaning

4. Think and judge independently and critically

5. Understand, interrogate and apply a variety of theoretical positions and weigh the importance of alternative perspectives.

C. PRACTICAL SKILLS

On completion of the programme the successful student will have a range of practical skills:

1. Use bibliographic skills, including accurate citation of sources and consistent use of conventions in the presentation of scholarly work

2. Demonstrate advanced literacy and communicative skills, including the ability to present sustained and persuasive written and oral arguments

3. Show competence in the planning and execution of essays and project-work

4. Demonstrate research skills, including information retrieval, organisation and critical evaluation.

Using learning outcomes as you study

To benefit from stated learning outcomes you need to check, as with assessment criteria, how the expectations they describe apply to or are reflected in the course or paper you are taking. The extent of overlap between the learning outcomes presented here and the assessment criteria listed above should not come as a surprise. What you are examined on should, after all, closely reflect the aims of the course you are studying and what you can reasonably be expected to have achieved by the end.

The learning outcomes presented above relate to undergraduate degree work; some of the expectations described are pitched higher than otherwise broadly equivalent assessment criteria as stated earlier, which reflect A Level courses as well. For example, you are expected at degree level to have more to say about how literary-critical ideas and trends shape value judgement. And as well as developing your own readings and setting them in a context, you are now expected to show awareness of more abstract, descriptive and theoretical systems for thinking about literary texts and their reception. Greater emphasis is also placed on following scholarly conventions in presenting your work. These differences are significant, and mark a shift of emphasis from literary studies at school into literary studies at university.

FAQS ABOUT HOW YOU ARE MARKED

While assessment criteria and learning outcomes can help you plan and monitor progress with your essay, it is also possible to be distracted from productive work by anxieties about marking. To help clear up areas of doubt, here are some frequently asked questions (FAQs) about marking, with some suggested answers.

Will assessment criteria stop me being original?

If you try to navigate your essay through highly specific assessment criteria you may wonder what scope is left for creativity or originality. This reaction is understandable, but underestimates how problematic any simple idea of **originality** is in literary studies. Unless you are doing advanced research, you are unlikely to be in a position to put forward new facts or radically new interpretations, or even to have enough knowledge of what other people have written to be sure you aren't duplicating what has been said before. This is especially likely with short essays and exam answers. In such cases, you cannot be expected to be 'original' in the way a researcher or expert in the field might be.

Faced with the challenge of being original in this ambitious sense, you may come to feel that, rather than trying to find something modest of your own to say, it would be better simply to copy or adapt someone else's work. This is inappropriate for several reasons, however: first, because you are often assessed on relative quality ('good for a second-year dissertation'), rather than absolute quality; second, because there is no point simply rewriting someone else's ideas (you might as well submit their book or article instead); and third, because it underestimates the scale of disagreement and change that exist in all areas of the field. Directly reproducing the work of established authors in your essay, even in order to pay homage to their originality, is not an accepted mode of writing essays or dissertations in (for example) British colleges and universities. Where sources are not properly acknowledged, this mode of writing is considered to be plagiarism (see Unit 13).

Rather than retreat from the problem of originality into copying other people's work, it is better to develop a more realistic sense of how you *can* be original, even in a short essay. You are expected to be – and can be – original in the sense of using your own knowledge and independent judgement to argue a case that derives from or builds on your own engagement with a text. Your case gains its originality from how you compare and weigh existing arguments in relation to the text or texts being discussed and in relation to your own reading, as well as by your choice of different examples from those to be found in works you have read or lectures you have attended.

Will I get blamed for expressing my opinion?

Another problem that arises from the difficulty of achieving a balance between being original and reproducing established material concerns how far it is acceptable to say that you are expressing your own opinion. Many students mistakenly believe that they shouldn't express their own opinion at all, and link this belief to a general instruction sometimes given – also inappropriately – that they should never use the first person pronoun 'I'.

Your own opinion is an essential part – though only one part – of your essay. Literary studies, as we have seen above, is a process of examining your own reactions to texts, describing but also trying to explain them. Your response to a text and opinions about it should be explored in a sort of dialogue with what you know about the historical context in which the text was written, the history of the text's reception and critical comment about it. Other possible reactions to the text should be taken into account, as should, where appropriate, more general theories about literary response and interpretation.

Will I be marked down for including general background material?

As the assessment criteria above make clear, what markers mean by a 'good' answer is typically one which is focused on the question or topic; one which is supported with textual evidence or other relevant illustration; and one which is coherently argued and written. Part of what makes an essay appear well focused and well argued is a sense that the material presented has been selected from a larger store of information you are in control of, which you are manipulating and deploying in order to present a particular argument you want to make.

Even where suitable evidence or illustration is lacking, markers will still look for something that is in some sense an answer to the question, or at least attempts to be. Evidence of engaging with the question will be sought in how far the question has been 'translated' into your own understanding, its terms reworked and the relationship between them investigated.

Markers tend to assign lower grades, including fail grades, to essays which fail to demonstrate that they are engaging with the terms of the question or topic. Commonly this is where information is presented without any indication that it has been selected to support a particular point, rather than merely reproduced, or where all that is offered is a simple description of what happens in the book or a rehash of what someone else has written about it.

IMAGINING YOUR READER AS SOMEONE PARTICULAR

In this final section, we return to the question of whether, even when you have access to explicit assessment criteria, there might still be a value in imagining your reader as someone specific. Every act of speaking or writing involves an **addressee**, the person you are speaking to or writing for. This addressee is either real or imagined, and guides the various linguistic choices the speaker or writer spontaneously makes. Writing an essay without even an *imaginary* addressee in mind may well lead to unplanned shifts of style and inconsistencies as regards what you take for granted and what you feel is worth saying.

Creating in your mind a **notional addressee** for your essay (that is, an addressee who is not a specific person) presents new difficulties, however. For example, you spend a great deal of time piecing together material for your essay, most of which will already be completely familiar to the only reader you have, your examiner. This oddity of the contrived relationship between the writer and reader of essays in literary studies makes it especially difficult to decide what kinds of information you should presuppose and what kinds of information you should present as being new. In Unit 9 we consider presupposition and problems of given and new information in detail. Here we need only say that keeping a notional addressee in mind sometimes helps resolve the difficulty of finding a suitable mode of address for your essay. For reasons very different from those with which we started, therefore, your tutor may be a suitable person to imagine you are addressing. Sometimes imagining you are speaking to a tutor can guide you towards an overall style appropriate to your field of study. You may also find it easier to attribute to such a person the unusual state of mind of wanting to be told in a full and careful way what he or she already knows. A large part of the craft of writing assessed essays in literary studies involves managing this peculiarity of who they are addressed to.

EXERCISE

Consider the following description of the expected characteristics of candidates who will be awarded the highest grade of pass in an exam. Such candidates, we are told,

> ...demonstrate a comprehensive, detailed knowledge and understanding of a wide range of literary texts from the past to the present, and of the critical concepts associated with literary study. Their discussion of texts shows depth, independence and insight in response to the tasks set, and they analyse and evaluate the ways in which form, structure and language shape meanings. Where appropriate, candidates identify the influence on texts of the cultural and historical contexts in which they were written. They are able to make significant and productive comparisons between texts which enhance and extend their readings, and are sensitive to the scope of their own and others' interpretations of texts. Their material is well organised and presented, making effective use of textual evidence in support of arguments. Written expression is fluent, well-structured, accurate and precise, and shows confident grasp of appropriate terminology.

In this unit we have suggested that assessment criteria are best understood not as personal attributes but as qualities in written essays for which there can be evidence. 'Translate' the above statement, which is expressed as an identikit image of a sort of person, into a list of qualities you might look for in a written essay. Alongside each quality, add a note of specific features in the writing or organisation of an essay that you could look for as evidence of it.

SELECTING PRIMARY AND SECONDARY TEXTS

Let's say you have decided on an author you wish to write about; now you have to choose a text or texts by that author to work on, either from among those you already know or by reading new ones. For a literary essay, these works will be what are traditionally called your **primary texts**, the literary texts your essay is basically about. **Secondary texts** are those other works which are relevant to your main project, and which you will use to support your analysis of the primary texts. Secondary texts might include other literary texts, diaries or letters, works of biography or history, or works of criticism and literary theory. In this unit we consider how to find and choose such works; in the next unit we look in more detail at how secondary sources support your research into any given topic.

HOW TO CHOOSE YOUR PRIMARY TEXTS

Choosing your primary texts appropriately is, in itself, a major step towards success in writing an essay. Which texts you choose, and how many, will actively shape the essay you produce. You might, for example, choose works you consider representative in some respect (e.g. typical of a genre, period or theme); or best known works (which you think need fresh attention); or little known or neglected, 'minor' works (which may need discovery or rehabilitation). Your choice between these different kinds of texts needs to be consistent with the overall purpose of the essay topic you are proposing. There is little point choosing Thomas Hardy's well-known novel *Far From The Madding Crowd* and arguing that this work is neglected and deserves to be known more widely.

Having chosen a text, you are likely to use it by focusing on one or more selected parts, either sections of the text (such as the beginning or a key episode) or aspects of the text (such as its narrative, or treatment of a particular theme). Where you have a free choice, it is often useful to focus on sections of a text which are of particular significance for functional reasons (because they are the first or last things a reader reads): the title, the beginning and the ending. A comparison between the first and last sentence might help you engage with the text and a wide range of problems it presents.

Choosing an edition

Many texts exist in more than one **edition**, usually printed at different times and sometimes by different publishers. Editions can differ both in trivial and in important ways. Trivial differences do not affect the text itself, and include differences in pagination or very minor printing corrections or errors. More important differences usually result from intervention by a specialist editor, who may change the text itself.

Whenever you choose a text, you are inevitably choosing an edition of that text, so look inside the front or sometimes back cover for the specific details of that edition. You should be interested in which edition you choose for at least three reasons.

1. Two different editions of what seems to be the same text can be different in important ways. For example the two editions of *Under Milk Wood* cited below differ in whether the voice-over narration is split between two narrators (the 2000 edition) or given to a single narrator (the 1994 edition).

> Thomas, D. 2000. *Under Milk Wood*. (edited by W. Davies)
> London: Penguin.
> Thomas, D. 1994. *Under Milk Wood*. (edited by W. Davies and
> R. Maud) London: Dent.

2. Some editions are considered more serious or scholarly than others, and you should try to use an edition which has some general legitimacy. This will often be referred to as an 'authorised', 'standard', 'authoritative' or 'critical' edition (see below for discussion of the features of such editions). It is worth remembering that the legitimacy of an edition may be disputed, though often such disputes are likely to be invisible to you. Unless you have a particular reason to use them, avoid free editions that you can get on the internet unless they are clearly indicated as critical editions, and avoid 'abridged' editions (i.e. choose 'unabridged') or newly illustrated editions for the popular (often children's) market. Editions in a college or university library are usually editions that will be accepted as legitimate; but check for the features indicated above.

3. By including details of the edition you are using, you help the reader of your work to locate that edition if they need to. For example, they might want to read further from a text you quote (perhaps to see its context more fully). Giving the edition of a text is also a way of offering a guarantee that you have quoted or summarised accurately. If you quote from the text using page numbers (as you should), the page numbers will vary depending on the edition, which is another reason to record which edition you are using.

Where the choice of edition is significant, you may wish to show in your writing that you are aware of the issues that surround your choice (some of these issues will probably be explained in the edition's introductory 'Note on the Text'). If you read with such issues in mind – how they actively affect what sense you can make of a text – introductory notes that may initially seem pedantic or irrelevant often become interesting in unexpected ways.

KINDS OF PRIMARY TEXT AND HOW TO USE THEM

Some editions, we have said, are considered more serious or legitimate than others: 'authorised', 'standard', 'authoritative' or 'critical' editions. But such editions are not all of one kind, and can serve slightly different purposes. We should therefore consider the features and usefulness of each kind.

Critical edition

The best edition to use, if available, is a **critical edition**. This will have a named editor, an introduction, a note on the text, and perhaps an index. Sometimes it will form part of a numbered, multi-volume edition published by a University Press. One disadvantage of such a critical edition, however, is that there is so much extra material surrounding the text that there is some danger of your relation with the text itself being disrupted. The opposite problem holds for a facsimile edition, as we now explain.

Facsimile edition

A **facsimile** of a text is an exact copy (usually a photographed copy) of a text, reprinted as a new book. Facsimiles have an inherent interest in that they give you some sense of what a book looked like when it was new; what, for example, the first edition of Wordsworth and Coleridge's *Lyrical Ballads* felt like in your hands, how big the pages were, what kind of font was used. Facsimiles can also record other aspects of the original; sometimes the first owner of a book writes in it, and these annotations may be carried over into a facsimile edition. For example, in a facsimile published by Scolar Press of Alexander Pope's *An Epistle from Mr Pope to Dr Arbuthnot*, the original 1734 owner Edward Harley has added notes to explain who all the people mentioned in the poem are.

Electronic edition

An 'electronic' edition of a text is one which can be accessed as a computer file. You might obtain it from a CD or DVD, or down-load it from the internet. You can find electronic versions of texts by using a search engine (e.g. Google TM) and typing in the first five or so words of the text, or often just the title. Many pre-twentieth century texts (because copyright restrictions no longer hold in such texts) are available on the internet, sometimes on sites specific to a writer or period, or in large general anthologies. Whole novels may be available, perhaps broken down into chapters. It is usually not a good idea to rely on an electronic text as your primary version of a text, however, since in most cases this will not be as 'legitimate' as a critical printed edition. There are, nevertheless, some interesting uses to which electronic versions of texts can be put.

An electronic version of a text is a searchable version. You could download Jane Austen's novel *Persuasion* and search the entire text for every time the word 'persuade' or 'persuasion' is used; then you could use that information as the basis for an analysis of the notion of persuasion in the novel and an explanation of the novel's title. An electronic version of a text is also a manipulable version. Some eighteenth-century critics thought that Milton's *Paradise Lost* was really prose converted into lines by simply being rewritten; you could experimentally test this claim by taking an electronic version of part of the poem and removing all the line boundaries, thus easily turning visual verse into visual prose. You could then try to reconstruct the line boundaries once more, and so find out how far the text's lineation is more than just layout on the page.

HOW TO CHOOSE SECONDARY TEXTS

Secondary texts, we have said, are texts that are relevant to your main project, and which you use to support your analysis of your chosen primary texts. Occasionally there are fundamentally important secondary texts that you must read and should refer to, such as a famous and influential critical essay on a particular text. But in general, there are few constraints on what you can use as secondary material in your writing so long as you establish its relevance. This lack of constraint can be a problem: there are so many possible secondary materials that to some extent you have to be lucky in discovering appropriate ones, even while being purposeful in selecting which materials to use.

The first thing to do is to open yourself up to luck, even if random wandering and searching clash with your idea of organised research. Actual wandering may be involved: going to a suitable library and scanning all the titles of books in the relevant section there, pulling any off the shelf for further inspection that look as if they may offer something. Bookshops offer the same possibility. You can also search documents, such as publishers' catalogues or anthologies of texts; and the internet presents possibilities for opening yourself up to luck, either using general search engines such as Google TM, or publishers' online catalogues, or online bookshops such as Amazon. Your goal in all of this is to make it possible for useful secondary reading to come to your attention. What these kinds of random wandering and searching also do is let you see the kinds and amount of secondary material which exist: what kinds of topics do people write on, when all you know is that they write about Virginia Woolf?

More systematic kinds of search are also possible. A book about an author will have a bibliography; in that bibliography there may be a book or a number of books you can use. For most short coursework essays, this may well be enough. But you can also use specialised bibliographies, and engage in what is called a **literature search** (where the word 'literature' just means 'anything written'). Many authors have whole bibliographies devoted to them, and there are bibliographies for particular subject areas (e.g. *Black British Literature. An annotated bibliography*). The most comprehensive bibliography for literary studies is the *Modern Language Association of America [MLA] International Bibliography*. Another, more selective and critical bibliography is *The Year's Work in Modern Language Studies*. ('Modern Language' in titles usually means literature as well as language.)

A third approach is to look at **abstracts**. An abstract is a short summary of content. For example, a yearly volume called *Abstracts of English Studies* gives short summaries of a large number of articles published in one year; there are indexes to help you find particular topics that have been written about. *Dissertation Abstracts International* is a collection of quite long abstracts of PhD dissertations. If you are writing a Master's or PhD dissertation, you should look at this collection to see what other people have written about the topic you are working on. You can use abstracts – either by accessing them in printed form or online – as a shop window of things to read, or you can just read and learn from the abstracts themselves.

Being selective

There is always more to read than you have time for. But one powerful principle of selection is forced on you: you can only use a book if you can get hold of it, usually either in your library or by interlibrary loan. Beyond availability, however, here are some other ways of being selective.

- Choose more recent books first (they may tell you what earlier books have said). Check book dates generally, and ask yourself whether a source may be giving you an outdated perspective.
- Look at the range of titles in the field, and for topics which keep coming up. Make sure you read at least one book on each relevant topic.
- If you have a book or article in your hands, check the contents page and preface or introduction; these will give you a sketch of the book's scope and argument. Look at its bibliography or index to see what it includes and what it misses out: how do the included topics fit with the sense of what is important that you have formed from what you have already read?
- Read the last page of the book or article; with any luck, it will summarise what went before, so you can choose whether to read the whole volume.
- Check the contents page, and try to link up the entries into a developing narrative or argument.

We should also repeat here a point we made in Unit 1. If you have already started to write your essay *before* you search for secondary reading then you will have a much better idea of what to look for, because you will already have begun to shape your argument and will have a sense of where you need to look for help.

KEEPING NOTES ON YOUR READING

There are two good reasons for keeping notes. First, doing so helps you pay attention to the text; by writing notes you are forced to think about what the text is saying. This is an advantage of notes even if you subsequently throw them away (and incidentally is also a good reason for taking notes in classes or lectures). Second, taking notes helps record what you have read, and in particular keeps a record of which page (and edition of a text) you found something useful on, so you can go back to it later.

Notes are more useful when they are short. It is rarely helpful to copy large sections of text, and it is usually better to start summarising and making what you are learning from your reading as concise as possible. Think about how much essay text will be given over to the material you get from this secondary source; usually you will write just a few sentences, and this should help constrain you in not taking more than you need from an original text. In case you decide to refer to a particular passage, it is essential that each note you make is accompanied by an accurate record of where the passage can be found, with sufficient information that you can complete a bibliographical reference. One of the most common accidental sources of plagiarism (see Unit 13) is when you take a note and do not record that what you have written is someone else's words; if you then incorporate the words of your note into your essay without referring to the original source you have in effect 'stolen' it.

EXERCISES

1. Choose one literary text that you might work on which is *representative* plus one which is *well known* plus one which is *neglected*. Explain why each text might be interesting to work on. (They don't have to be by the same author.)

2. Choose a book and a key word. For example you might choose Charlotte Bronte's *Jane Eyre* and 'romance', or Shakespeare's *Hamlet* and 'suicide'. Now, using any of the 'wandering and searching' techniques described in this unit, find three secondary texts (articles or books) whose titles suggest that they would be relevant to an essay on this book and this topic.

3. Read a critical essay, and make notes about it. (Ideally, use a critical essay that can be used as secondary reading for an essay you are actually writing.) The constraint is that you must use no more than a single side of paper for all the notes you take. (This will give you practice in being concise.)

GETTING HELP FROM REFERENCE WORKS, ONLINE RESOURCES AND YOUR SUPERVISOR

In the previous unit, we showed how to find and select texts. These included secondary texts that enable you to link your analysis of the main literary works you are studying to other kinds of research into your topic. In this unit we look more closely at the main kinds of learning resources that are likely to be useful to you, and how to make the most of help you can get from reference works and other sources including your supervisor.

USING SECONDARY TEXTS

The secondary texts you might use can be divided into three kinds: research publications; books written for students (textbooks); and self-published work (which includes most websites).

Research publications

Research publications, if they are books, are generally **monographs** (that is, specialist books on a specific topic), or are published as articles in journals. Published articles of this kind usually go through a 'refereeing' process, where first versions are evaluated by reviewers, who may reject them or require them to be changed before they can be published. Published articles (and to a lesser extent monographs) have in this way gone through a quality check, which should ensure that they are reliable and serious pieces of work. Ideally, you should try to read some work of this kind, and should aim to imitate the style and mode of this kind of writing in your essays or dissertations.

Research articles are published in journals, and can be at any level of specialisation. It is worth going to your library, where journals are probably kept in a separate section called 'Periodicals'; find a relevantly titled journal and spend an hour or so scanning the journal indexes, looking at the title of every article published in the past decade. As well as possibly presenting some relevant articles to you, this process will give you a sense of the kind of things people write. Some journals publish overview articles; for example *Victorian Poetry* has a yearly set of articles that discuss a large number of publications published in the area over the past year. Some journals publish copies of their articles online, either making them freely available or through a subscription from your library.

Textbooks

Textbooks are generally reliable for the purpose of coursework essays. For economic reasons, many publishers are reluctant to publish academic books unless they can be considered to have a potential appeal to students, and this means that a potential monograph can sometimes end up written as a textbook. It is never a good idea, however, to rely entirely on books addressed primarily to students; you should attempt to read and refer to work addressed to a specialist academic readership as well. When you are writing your essay, be careful not to imitate the style of textbooks, which for example may put technical terms in boldface as an aid to the reader (see Unit 10). You should try instead to approximate more closely to the style of research publications; the more advanced your level of study, the less use you are likely to make of textbooks, except in early stages of familiarising yourself with an area.

There are various things you may be looking for when you use a textbook. You may want:

- background factual information, or explanations of difficult concepts;

- other people's interpretations of what you are reading;
- accepted areas for debate (to narrow down what you think you should discuss, in the light of what other people have chosen to talk about).

Self-published work

Self-published work is mainly found on the internet. Many internet publications and the content of most websites will not have gone through any process of quality control, and cannot therefore be considered reliable. This is a disadvantage that has to be set against the fact that internet publication is often undertaken by enthusiasts who have a commitment to what they are saying (though many other sites are put up by people with something to sell). Self-published internet work can be valuable to you, but should be treated with caution.

REFERENCE BOOKS

The Oxford English Dictionary

A word may have a different meaning when it occurs in a different place (e.g. 'cot' means a child's bed in British English but also a bed for adults in Indian English), or at a different time (e.g. 'gentle' used to carry the meaning of 'upper class', as in 'gentry', but now can be used as an approving description – something like 'sensitive' – of *anyone's* character). Because words change in meaning, it can be particularly useful to use a historical dictionary such as the *Oxford English Dictionary* (also called the **OED**; it exists as a multi-volume set, or photographically reduced, or online, or on CD-ROM). The full version of this dictionary lists all the meanings a word has had, with quotations to illustrate them. Other helpful dictionaries are ones that contain lists of words which have special meanings in literary criticism, such as *The Princeton Encyclopedia of Poetry and Poetics* or *A Handlist of Rhetorical Terms*.

Concordances

A **concordance** is a list of all the words used by a particular author, with an indication of where those words are to be found. You can use a concordance to find a particular place in a text if you know a word used there, or as a way of following up a particular theme, metaphor or symbol. For example, if you look up the word 'wit' in a *Concordance to the Plays of William Congreve*, you will find all the places where the seventeenth-century dramatist Congreve used that word; you can then work out what the particular meaning of that word must have been for Congreve by studying how he uses it in a range of settings. Most libraries will, at a minimum, have a concordance to the King James (1611) version of the Bible (and you can buy these fairly cheaply secondhand); this concordance will help you track down allusions to and quotations from the Bible, which are very common in many literary works in English.

Biographies and handbooks

If you are writing about a twentieth-century author and want ideas about the author or what to say about her or him, you have a range of options. You could use the massive reference work published by Gale, *Contemporary Authors* (which lists biographical and bibliographical information, together with other relevant comments), or *Contemporary Literary Criticism*, which describes itself as 'excerpts from criticism of the works of today's novelists, poets, playwrights and other creative writers'. Some authors you are interested in may be less well-documented in traditional information sources such as these, for example pre-twentieth century women authors; in such cases you may find it useful to use the *Dictionary of British Women Writers*. On the other hand, better-known authors may have specialised sources of information devoted to them, such as *A D.H. Lawrence Handbook*.

Sometimes you may find that you have access to a text, but not to all the information you would like about it. You may have seen a film, but wish to discuss who did the cinematography or who played a particular character. Once the film credits are over, you have no permanent record. In this case, as an alternative to hiring a DVD where available, you can use a popular reference work like *Halliwell's Film Guide*, or a journal like *The Monthly Film Bulletin* or *Sight and Sound*. There are also more specialised information sources you may need to use. If you wish to know about the readership for a particular contemporary magazine or newspaper, for example (perhaps as part of a study of the relation between ideology and audience), you could use *BRAD* ('British Rate and Data'): alongside prices for advertising, this work lists audited newspaper and magazine circulations, and is a useful extra source when working with newspaper or magazine articles that you can find in your library or online.

Historical information

Sometimes it is historical information that will be useful. Here, various reference sources are available including an **annals** (a book which groups events by year). If you are writing about Eliot's poem *The Waste Land*, published in 1922, for example, you might consider it relevant to know about other events during that year, so you could look up 1922 in an annals, or in some other kind of reference source such as the index to the newspaper *The Times* (a London newspaper suited to the fact that the poem is set partly in London, and was published there). In these indexes you will find information about types of event (e.g. crimes), about the arts (e.g. reviews) and about the subjects and terms of reference of contemporaneous public debate. As well as indexes for many newspapers, there are compendia (or collections) like *Keesing's Contemporary Archives* ('factual reports on current affairs throughout the world, based on information abstracted from press, broadcasting, official and other sources', published from 1931 onwards).

Tracking down allusions

Sometimes a novel or poem gains some of its meaning by quoting or referring to another text. In these cases, writers may expect their readers instantly to recognise such **allusions**. But there are inevitably changes in what readers know automatically, even leaving aside questions of education, social background, gender, ethnicity or age. A person in 2005 will have a different store of knowledge from a person in 1905, and even more different from a person in 1805. So information sources are needed to stand in for what we do not automatically know. If you suspect a text may be quoting another text, you can check by looking up what you take to be the key word of the possible quotation in a Dictionary of Quotations. If you think an allusion is being made to a Greek or Roman myth, you can try *Lempriere's Classical Dictionary* or some other dictionary of Classical mythology. If you think a reference is being made to the Bible, you can use a concordance to the Bible in an analogous way. In some cases, the searching has been done for you by previous scholars; for example there is a book called *Allusions in Ulysses* (which lists allusions made in James Joyce's novel *Ulysses*). Alongside such specialised resources, you can always use general-purpose encyclopedias or a search engine like Google TM, which may provide clues about what field to look in for further information even though these sources are unlikely themselves to be the end-point of your search.

Other useful sources

Finally, there are books that have information about many different kinds of topic, and which can turn out to be useful in unpredictable ways. These include *The Oxford Companion to Literature*, where you will find information about authors, texts, literary movements, and general historical facts. *The Oxford Illustrated History of English Literature* allows you to explore literary history by comparing commentary, quotation and pictures. *The Cambridge Encyclopedia of the English Language* and *The Cambridge Encyclopedia of Language* are comprehensive and accessible sources of information about language, including language in literature. The original (but still available) *Brewer's Dictionary of Phrase and Fable* is an example of a nineteenth-century collection of somewhat idiosyncratically chosen historical, mythical and literary information; it is useful partly because of its eccentricity, in that it contains information you may well not find elsewhere. And it would be wrong to overlook the very large general encyclopedias like *Encyclopedia Britannica*, again available either in multi-volume book form, online or on DVD-ROM. Even if, for example, you wish to know about what you consider highly specialised subjects such as punctuation in the seventeenth century, marriage laws in nineteenth-century Canada, the history of the Elizabethan stage, or current theories of myth or symbol, this is still a place worth looking. Ignore the scepticism of those obsessed with 'definitive' sources: the entries in *Britannica* are always good, and often surprisingly detailed.

KEEPING REFERENCES

When you write, you use what other people have written. One of the conventions of research is that you must enable your reader to find again what you yourself have read. That is partly why in the previous unit we emphasised the importance of keeping notes of where you found something (of course it is also useful for *you* to be able to find again what you have read). Your notes need to record enough details of a book, article or other source to enable it to be found again. In some cases it can be difficult or even sometimes impossible to find texts again (for example if the text is a lecture); but you should still keep details as fully as possible, so your reader knows exactly where ideas or words came from.

The information you need to keep for everything you read includes the following. (You will find such information usually at the beginning of a book – though some books have details of publication on the last page instead.)

1. The author's full name. Underline the family name, since this is the part that decides where it will go in an alphabetical list.

2. Any other people involved, besides the author. There might for example be an editor, compiler or translator.

3. The full title – and subtitle – of the work. Put a colon between the title and the subtitle, even if there isn't one in the original. Underline the title of a book, and put an article's title in single quotation marks.

4. The name of the publisher, the place where it was published, and the date of publication – all for the edition you have in your hands. Often books will have a list of different places; the convention is to choose only the first. In some cases you may want to add further information: books are published in Cambridge UK and also in Cambridge USA, so just saying 'Cambridge' may in some cases not be enough; add country details where you think there may be a possibility of confusion.

5. If the text is an article in a journal or a chapter in an edited book or anthology, keep details about the collection you found it in; for a journal article, note the volume and issue number, and the page numbers for the article.

6. Sometimes books or articles exist in several different versions. If you are not using the original version, you should say so (e.g. by noting 'second edition' or 'reprinted version' or 'facsimile'). You should keep details of the original version, if you can find them. For an article in an anthology, you need to keep details of the journal it was originally published in. For a facsimile edition note information relating to the current edition and also information relating to the original edition. If a book is a translation, keep information about the original title, publisher, etc.

7. Usually you will refer to or quote from a particular place in a book or article; note the page number. Because literary texts exist in different editions it is sometimes more helpful to note the chapter number, act and scene number, line number, etc. (and of course, you should indicate the exact edition you are using).

8. For a website, keep a note of the exact internet address (the URL) and the date you consulted it, because internet sites can change (or disappear) at any time; if possible, and if it is legal for you to do so, keep a copy of the internet page for reference.

9. For your own benefit, you may find it worth keeping a record of where *you* found a particular book (which library, and the call number), in case you need to consult it there again.

READING WHAT YOU FOUND

Finding a book or article is of course only the beginning. Once you have the text in your hands, there are a number of different ways of using it. Because you will often have more to read than you have time for, you need to develop ways of reading more quickly and efficiently. The techniques of scanning and skimming can both be used to gain a rough idea of what an article or book contains, so you can read parts in more detail later if you want to. You can **scan**: this kind of reading involves looking quickly at each page, to pick out anything you recognise as being relevant to you, which you will then read in detail; scanning involves looking for keywords. Or you can **skim**: this involves reading the first sentence of each paragraph, and anything prominent or highlighted; in this case, it is the general sense and flow of the book you are trying to absorb.

Both of these reading techniques are examples of how reading is a selective activity. Even when you **read intensively** (that is, you focus on every word) you are still inevitably selective in what you understand or absorb. If you read an article or book twice you will probably be surprised by how many new things you discover the second time. It is a common experience that you get new ideas when you try to write about something you have read; so you read the original again and suddenly see new things in it because of the new ideas you have brought to it. This common experience suggests that books or articles that are important to your project should be read more than once (early on, and then again later in your study). Reading is an active process, one where what you bring affects what you get out of the text; and the more you know, the more you can understand. Don't go to books passively, expecting simply to absorb and be informed. Constantly ask yourself: what question is reading this book going to help with? As you read through a book or long article, pause after each chapter or section and look back at any notes you have taken. Do they make sense? Do they provide facts or views you can use? Are there particular points you need to go back to, or will need to find out more about?

LEARNING BY BEING SUPERVISED

Writing essays and dissertations can be an isolated or even lonely experience, but it usually takes place in a structured environment, typically a school, college or university. Alongside all the printed and online reference resources you can use, therefore, you can also seek help from a teacher; for a dissertation, this teacher is likely to be called your 'supervisor'. How much tutorial support you are offered will vary from course to course; what we focus on here is how to make the most of whatever support is available.

Supervision in some academic subjects – such as some science subjects – involves very clear direction and close monitoring by your supervisor, who is likely to give you a topic to work on. In literary studies, by contrast, this arrangement would be unusual; a supervisor for a literary essay or dissertation will generally respond to the work you produce rather than telling you specifically what you must do. This is partly because literary studies is unlikely to involve a group of students working as a team towards a common goal. It is also because literary studies, more than most subjects, requires you to draw on your own resources, reflect on your own readings, and generate your own enthusiasms, bringing into your work an interest that will motivate you to read, generate ideas and write. Inventiveness and boldness, which often accompany enthusiasm, are usually encouraged and rewarded. This all means that a supervisor must maintain a careful balance between encouraging you to work on your own, as creatively as possible, and at the same time keeping you on track in terms of the standards by which you will be assessed.

The implication for you is that you will need to find ways of making the best use of your supervisor, rather than assuming that your supervisor will provide a ready-made structure of work for you. This can include explicit negotiation as to what you can expect from each other. It may also mean preparing an informal agenda for each supervision meeting. Towards the end of each supervisory session, you should check that you have understood what was discussed and have noted down what now needs to be done. More than anything else, preparing for a supervision means doing some writing in advance, and giving it to your supervisor so that they can read it before they see you. If for some reason this arrangement for before your meeting breaks down, then it is worth asking your supervisor to read through what you have written with you (if it's not too long) during the supervision itself.

Supervision in literary studies can sometimes run into a problem that is probably more common in this discipline than in others. Most supervisors will put more effort into identifying what they think are your mistakes or what still needs to be done, and less effort into praising your successes. What makes this particularly sensitive in literary studies is that you are likely to have put more of yourself into the work – your own readings, your own ideas, your own emotional responses – and so criticism of your work can feel like criticism of you. If you are upset by a supervision, or by comments written on your work, we suggest that you talk to the supervisor/marker about it. A common, and sometimes reassuring explanation is that your supervisor has not realised that her or his comments, intended to improve your work, could have upset or annoyed you.

EXERCISES

1. Pick a pre-twentieth-century text (either a poem, novel or play, at least 100 lines long) that you already have access to in a printed form. Look for an electronic version of the text on the internet (if you can't find one, try a different text). Download it. Choose a key word or phrase, and search for this word or phrase in the text.

2. (If you have access to a library which keeps 'periodicals' or 'journals'.) Pick an author, and find a journal whose title suggests that it may include articles on that author. Spend about 30 minutes scanning the titles – or possibly the contents – of articles published in the journal, to find articles which mention or discuss your author (even if as part of a more general discussion). Try to find at least three.

THE FIRST DRAFT

Planning an essay is one thing; actually starting to write one is another. If you look at your first blank screen or page and freeze, how will you unfreeze yourself and get started? In this unit we look at some ways of doing this. The governing principle is that essays need to be constructed as much as written. So while it can seem a good idea to start writing a full draft as soon as possible, there are other kinds of preparatory writing that are worth doing first. Time spent on an initial synopsis and outline, establishing an essay's structure, reduces problems of shape and proportion when the essay is written in full.

STARTING TO WRITE

One productive starting point is to break the illusion that writing is a 'gestation' process, in which you wait for inspiration until the essay forms itself, fully-fledged, in your mind and just needs to be written down. Even in exams, as we suggested in Unit 2, some initial planning and rough drafting are needed before you start the main process of composition. In general, we repeat, it is a good idea to start writing as soon as you can. But your first attempts will not necessarily feel like you are writing your essay 'proper'.

It is always a good idea, for example, to write a one-paragraph **synopsis** (a summary of the essay) before working on a full draft. That synopsis is in effect a joined-up version of your earlier note-form statement of essay focus and mode of argument (see Unit 3). A useful test for your synopsis is to imagine you are at a party and someone asks you what you are writing about: your answer has to be short, coherent and sufficiently interesting to hold the attention of a listener who is not obliged to listen to you and doesn't necessarily know anything about your chosen topic. The answer most suited to such circumstances offers a useful shape for your synopsis. When you have produced it, keep your synopsis handy whenever you are writing, and edit it periodically. Writing your argument down will probably change that argument, so it is likely – and sometimes unavoidable – that you will change your synopsis as you progress. This doesn't reduce its worth. Your synopsis is needed to start you off and then later as a reference point, something easily modified to reflect your evolving ideas.

Be willing to do disposable work. Versions which you know you are going to throw away at some point allow you to experiment in ways you wouldn't risk in a draft you consider 'final' or 'near final'. By thinking that everything is final – that it must pass your own 'quality control' test – you even reduce the likelihood of producing any work at all. Drafting and re-drafting allows lower-intensity and less stressful work than packing everything into a single, decisive act of composition. Break the process of constructing an essay down into easier, small steps. Note your arguments on a piece of paper. They look wrong. You edit the notes, making them clearer or more coherent. The next day, you come at the same problems with a fresh eye (or at least from a slightly different angle). The notes look wrong again – but this time for slightly different reasons. You do further editing. The text evolves, through successive steps of minor re-drafting rather than through the more mysterious process of gestation. Importantly, with drafting there is less chance of outside events or circumstances making you forget where you've got to.

Make a timetable. Step-by-step writing allows you to do this, and commits you to making progress, even if you later discard what you have done. Bear in mind other commitments when outlining your programme of work (e.g. holidays, weekends, need for rest, etc.). Be realistic from the outset, so that you don't become dismayed by inability to keep to your own timetable.

Develop strategies to help 'unlock' the process of writing when you get stuck. Sometimes you may need to write each main point in your argument on a separate card or sheet of paper and physically re-order them on a table in front of you, joining up the points in your mind with a linking commentary. How do you get from this point to this? What is it that makes you want to put this point before that one? The value of having such materials in brief and physically separate forms is that it is easier to manipulate ideas while they are still in note form than it is once you have written them out in prose.

KEEPING TO A GIVEN FORMAT

It is essential to think ahead as you write, practically as well as in terms of your argument. Consider the essay's overall length and the length of the various parts it will consist of. Where you can, consult essays already successfully submitted. Just as you can prepare for an exam by looking at old exam questions, you can prepare to write an essay project or dissertation by looking at examples that have been submitted and accepted by your institution. Looking at such examples should ensure that you are not completely ignorant of the scope, length or demands of what you are trying to do. It is possible to alter aspects of your essay's format right up to the moment you hand it in, but with length and other major considerations it is better to work to an appropriate format from the outset, rather than repair problems afterwards.

Length and proportion

How much will you be expected to write? You may find that your course, college or university has rules for upper and lower limits, so check these before you start; but the figures in Table 1 gives some idea.

If you aren't using a word-processor with a word-count facility, there is little point counting every word. An estimate is enough. Work out an average number of words per line and lines per page; multiplying your page-average by the number of pages gives a rough total that should tally adequately with tutors' estimates and

Table 1 Typical essay lengths

Number of words	Project type	Number of A4 pages
1,200–1,500	coursework task	3–4 hand-written
2,000–2,500	essay	5–6 hand-written; 8–10 double-spaced type-written
5,000	undergraduate project	20–25 double-spaced type-written
10,000–15,000	more extended, or 'double-weight' undergraduate dissertation	40–75, double-spaced type-written

impressions – they won't count individual words either. When you have noted the overall length you need to produce, use this to judge an equally important aspect of the essay to do with length: relative proportion between different sections. Divide the prescribed overall length into sections of suitable length, so that the essay will have a 'balance' as it develops, with worked-out proportions being given over to each stage. This balance should prevent you running out of space before completing what you want to say.

WRITING TO AN OUTLINE

Working on how topics interrelate in your essay, so that what comes first leads into what comes next, helps refine your argument, even when you have a synopsis. Matching steps in your argument to the essay's various sections requires further organisation, if you are to achieve a suitable balance between them and at the same time meet an overall length requirement. That task of organising your topics is made easier if before starting your first draft you construct a detailed **outline**.

You might, for instance, assign half a page to an introductory paragraph, and one page to a summary of what other people have said, with half a page kept back for conclusions. Such general proportions provide a sense of how much it is possible to say in each section. More importantly, if the essay becomes too long, an outline will show where deletions can be made, other than just cutting off the end or deciding not to write whichever sections don't yet exist. The material you should delete is just as likely to come from the middle sections as from the end: take out redundant or duplicated examples; cut lists shorter, reduce alternative words offered as glosses, etc. Selective cutting of this kind shortens your essay without losing its balance or structure.

Your outline will work better if it is genuinely a structure rather than a list. To see how this is achieved, consider this first version of an outline for an essay on the Scottish novelist Josephine Tey:

introduction
career as a London playwright
recent critical appraisal
powers of description
humour
education
church
the divided self
the divided self – most of all as a woman
her final novel – *The Singing Sands*

As it stands, this outline makes no attempt to show how the parts relate to each other, or what the development is from one to another, or even what the point is of some of the parts. Why, for example, should there be a special section devoted to her final novel but not the others?

We might begin the process of reorganising this draft outline like this:

introduction
biographical details (including career as a London playwright)
qualities as a writer
  – powers of description
  – humour

themes
   – education
   – church
   – the divided self
   – the divided self, most of all as a woman
recent critical appraisal
conclusion: her final novel – *The Singing Sands*

To get to this revised version from the original, we have introduced different levels of argument, and made the following organisational changes:

1. We put 'career as a London playwright' into a larger section called 'biographical details', because there are other biographical points we will want to make.

2. We grouped 'powers of description' and 'humour' in a section called 'qualities as a writer'; we can now add other qualities to this section if we wish. Similarly we created a group of 'themes'.

3. We moved 'recent critical appraisal' after our analysis of powers of description and humour, because these sections give our own critical appraisal; now, by the time we outline other people's opinions we have something to compare them with, and can therefore do something more interesting than just repeat them.

4. We have made explicit the reason for focusing on the last novel – we chose it because it acts as a summary of Tey's work, and so is an appropriate topic for a conclusion.

The two main techniques we have used here – grouping points into more general categories and introducing levels of argument – have turned a 'list' outline into an argument structure. As you introduce structure in this way, your attention will inevitably be drawn to unresolved or additional issues of sequence, or gaps or possible connections between points, and you will make further changes – constructing your argument by constructing your outline.

Like your synopsis, your outline will need to be modified as you write; you will continue to see fresh possibilities in how your various topics and sub-topics relate to each other. So long as you update your outline rather than leaving it behind, you will always have a model of the argument at hand that signals sequence, main connections between points, and the relative proportion of overall word-length you are devoting to each section. Each topic in your outline – that is, each step or topic in your argument – translates into a section of your essay, with its own appropriate length. In this way your outline links abstract properties of your argument with physical properties of your text. It should incidentally allow you to write the various parts of your essay in any order you like, without necessarily starting at the beginning and writing your way through.

Things to avoid in writing your outline

With a longer project or dissertation, be careful not to overload the first part, especially if the first part is a biographical summary, a description of historical context, or a literature review. All of these are potentially interminable, and distort the proportions of the essay as a whole.

To overcome such problems, try in particular to *avoid* the following structure, despite its apparent or commonsense attraction:

1. literature review;

2. introduce case study;

3. detail of case study;

4. analysis, findings and conclusion.

In this type of structure, 1. usually becomes overloaded. Instead, try something like this:

1. scene-setting; reasons for interest; the problem;

2. case study;

3. analysis of findings;

4. discussion of wider themes; relation to existing work.

In this revised format, material from your literature review is presented, paradoxically, towards the end (under 'relation to existing work'), where you examine implications and applications, rather than at the beginning.

Using 'outline view'

If you are writing on paper, your outline will be a separate document. This will be useful, but can make it difficult to use the outline as scaffolding for the process of writing besides using it as a reference point or checklist. To use a paper outline as a frame in which to draft material, you have to copy it across to a fresh document, or write out each heading on a new sheet of paper and draft relevant material on each sheet separately. Rearranging topics in your outline then means rearranging those sheets of paper. If you are using word-processing software, on the other hand, you can integrate your outline more fully into the process of drafting.

To use your outline as a tool in drafting, first write the outline on screen, roughly in the form of the second Josephine Tey example above. Then use the style formatting facility of a programme like Microsoft® Word to assign different styles to section titles at each level of argument (the different levels for headings were signalled in our example above by indentation: 'education' and 'church', for example, are both down a level from 'themes' and are indented one tab further to the right). In Microsoft® Word, the styles will be labelled, for example, Heading 1, Heading 2, Heading 3; and draft material you write under any heading will be in a style called something like Normal or Body Text. Using different views, you can now work either with all of your draft material in front of you, or with just the headings, showing their different levels as a skeleton of the argument. If in outline view you move headings up or down your document's running order, the text related to the heading you are moving moves with it. In this way you can reorganise whatever you have written by manipulating headings rather than by elaborate cutting and pasting. Switching between viewing the whole document and viewing only the outline enables you to move easily between the detailed wording of your argument and an overview of its structure; being able to see your argument from different points of view in this way is a powerful editing tool.

EXERCISE

Choose an essay title related to a novel you are currently studying. (If you do not have any titles, choose a title from earlier units in this book that relates to a work you are familiar with or adapt a question so that it fits a work you do know.) Brainstorm ideas for an essay in response to that title, without (to begin with) worrying about whether the points you think of are details, themes, arguments, etc. Now sort your points into a simple 'list' outline of the kind illustrated above. At this stage, you are just trying to find a likely order in which to introduce the points. Now work through your list, sorting the points into groups and introducing levels (e.g. general point, example, etc.). Finally, rearrange the points at the top level into the order that seems to answer the question most effectively; drag the points at lower levels into their new places in the outline.

DEVELOPING YOUR ARGUMENT

The underlying purpose of writing essays in literary studies is to **argue a case**, and in this unit we examine different ways of arguing that can be adopted. We focus in particular on how the kinds of argument for which you have produced a structure and an outline should hold together and develop internally. In Units 9–12, we look in more detail at writing and editing techniques with which you can present such arguments to best effect.

CAUSATION, CORRELATION AND COINCIDENCE

When you comment on a given passage, you claim some kind of connection between the features analysed and something else about the text, such as its meaning, its effect on a reader, how good it is, or its historical origins. In most cases, the connection is between observation (of structure) and response (your interpretation). Without observations, responses are mere impressions. Without responses or interpretation, on the other hand, observations are unworked-out descriptions. In between, there are different strengths of connection between these two aspects of reading, ranging from **causation**, through **correlation**, to **coincidence**.

Here is an example. You analyse a poem as having an especially regular rhyme scheme; you also find that the poem makes you feel cheerful. The crudest way to describe this is to say that it has 'a cheerful rhyme scheme'. But this fails to think properly about the relation between the rhyme scheme and the effect on you, which you can do by asking which of the following is true:

1. the rhyme scheme *causes* the cheerfulness. (This connection is the easiest to claim but also the least analysed; can it really be so simple?); or

2. there is a relationship between the rhyme scheme and the cheerfulness, but it is one of *correlation*; you think there is some connection between them such that you might expect them to be found together (but you are not sure yet what it is); or

3. the regular rhyme scheme is connected with the cheer-fulness because they are *both caused by something else* (such as the genre or subject matter of the poem, perhaps); or

4. there is in your view no relationship between the rhyme scheme and the feeling, and they *coincide* without there being a causal or correlative relation between them.

Coincidence is the least interesting case; it is also the most common. Causation, conversely, is likely to be the most interesting, but is also the most difficult to demonstrate. This is because, with a literary text, what is caused is often inside your head: an emotional response or impression of meaning. While such states are central to literary studies, it is difficult to describe them precisely; and for this reason, although they are of great interest, they are also inevitably weak points in your argumentation.

ASSEMBLING A DESCRIPTION OR COMMENTARY

The simplest form of essay organisation consists of just the presenta-tion of a commentary or series of descriptions. But what guides the sequence in which such descriptions are to be presented? One com-mon sequence is based on **chronology** (historical sequence), such as the development of a novelist's concerns throughout her lifetime. But there are other kinds of possible sequence, too, such as a text-by-text commentary on works in a collection (e.g. *Lyrical Ballads*); or you might recount events in a narrative, telling them to your reader in the order in which they happen.

If you organise your essay by imitating a sequence which already exists – such as the sequence in which a series of books were written – you are failing to take an opportunity: the opportunity to devise the most appropriate sequence to fit what you intend to say. In this kind of imitative sequence, the materials you have collected together (the events in the story, the biography of an author, etc.) are simply presented in the order in which they originally occur; and this generally produces uninteresting and unoriginal essays. No process of reworking, assimilation or re-presentation has taken place; there is little *added* by you.

CLASSIFICATION

Using the same information available for a sequential description, however, you can organise an essay in other, more interesting ways. You can demonstrate a process of re-ordering, and so your own contribution, by reshaping the material around an overall organising principle or generalisation. For example, one classificatory system that could be imposed on the material divides it into abstract categories (e.g. into a chronology on the basis of definable periods; or into a **typology**, or system of sorting on the basis of formal likeness and difference). Any classificatory system you use to organise your essay will have to be explained, of course (e.g. divisions between historical periods need to be discussed and justified). But introducing a classificatory element almost always radically improves a descriptive essay. It enables you to get straight into analysis and debate, leaving basic description to passages of supporting illustration; and it emphasises your point of view or commentary rather than mere repetition of materials possibly already available to your reader in their original form. Always ask yourself: why should anyone read my essay, when they could read the original text?

One fruitful form of classification starts from a **keyword** (sometimes a historical term, such as 'Restoration'; sometimes a conceptual term, such as 'nature'; sometimes a genre term, such as 'tragedy').

Consider the case of tragedy. If you are writing on this topic, you can work out a list of sorts of tragedy. This prompts you to do something else, namely to work out the relationship between the parts of the list: why are all the different sorts of tragedy called tragedy? What are the historical links and sequence between them? etc.

Classification is also useful when you are working with a text that has not been extensively discussed, but which relates to classifications which *have* been discussed. For example, if you choose to write an essay on a novel which was published last month, you may find it difficult to get any critical work either on the book itself or on the writer. But you can work out how this novel would fit into various classificatory systems, and then discuss the novel in relation to such frameworks: is its genre a suitable point of departure, or possibly the national culture within which it is written?

Classifications are often a basis for finding correlations. As an illustration of this, consider the following project.

An essay on metaphors used in advertisements. This project might begin with an analysis of the metaphors used in ten advertisements. We decide to look for a connection between types of advert and types of metaphor. In order to do this, we classify the adverts into types: 'aimed at women' and 'aimed at men' (we could instead have classified them as 'television' versus 'magazine' or 'Italian' versus 'British', etc.; and if our first attempt to classify gets us nowhere we might try one or more of these alternatives at a later stage). We then also classify the metaphors into types: 'metaphors where an object is treated like a part of a body' and 'other types of metaphor'. We are now in a position to ask whether one type of advert typically uses one type of metaphor. If the answer is 'yes', then we have learnt something (a correlation, which may turn out to be an instance of causation); and in writing it down we will be saying something new. If on the other hand the answer is 'no', then we eliminate this line of enquiry, and perhaps try one of the alternative classifications of adverts and metaphors suggested above.

PRESENTING ALTERNATIVE ARGUMENTS

In this mode of organising an essay, you divide the issue you are addressing into conflicting positions, or points of view, or sides of an argument. The structure of the essay becomes one of comparing claims made from differing viewpoints, and assessing the validity and appropriateness of each.

Sometimes you can shape your essay round an already-existing critical controversy (e.g. between established schools of thought, such as 'New Criticism' and 'Post-structuralism'). In order to accentuate the general significance of your arguments, it can be helpful to generalise from individuals to movements or types of thought (you discuss Leavisism, for instance, rather than F.R. Leavis's work in particular). In presenting ideas of a school or movement, however, you need to be careful to distinguish your own words from your paraphrase of the positions you are representing. Be explicit at the point where you leave off summarising and your own words take over (see Unit 13 for techniques which will help you do this). You will also need, in this type of essay, to signal that you are aware of the dangers of **reductionism**: that is, of simplifying the work of a school or movement until it no longer adequately represents what anyone associated with it would recognise or subscribe to.

EXPERIMENTING

A literary **experiment** changes a text and looks at how the change affects a reader. For example, you choose a narrative, then write a summary of a different ending for it, and think what implications the alternative ending would have. Such an experiment focuses on the writer's actual decision about an ending, but also begins to tell you about how endings work in general. Experiments of this kind can be simply 'thought experiments' (just imagine the ending), but because writing is always a way of thinking, we encourage you to write your ideas onto the page; the act of writing often reveals something new.

Most experiments in literary studies involve taking related versions of a text and seeing what effects on a reader result from differences between them. The selected texts (or versions of a single text) will be alike in many respects, yet different in perhaps one basic way – called the **variable**. You are likely to be looking for the relation between the variable part of the text (called the **independent variable** because you are manipulating it by making changes) and the variation in the response of the reader (called the **dependent variable**, because it depends on the variation, or changes, made to the text). One of the crucial rules about doing an experiment is to report it fully, so that it can be repeated if anyone wishes to. You also need to control the circumstances in which you conduct the experiment, in order as far as possible to eliminate conflicting or distracting variables (such as tiredness, lateness in the day, unequal difficulty of the texts used, etc.).

If your experiment involves other people (e.g. if you are comparing different readers' responses), you need to consider ethical issues which arise, including (i) getting their permission to use the results; (ii) showing them the results and explaining them; (iii) not using their names when you report the experiment (even if they have given permission for this, there is unlikely to be any point); (iv) the ethical problem that sometimes an experiment is best conducted if test subjects don't know what it is for; that is, if there is a 'secret agenda'. If your experiment involves large groups, then you also need to think about the significance of numerical results you may produce; for this, guidebooks about experimentation and the use of statistics may be needed.

PROVIDING CONTEXTS FOR TEXTS

Another form of argument involves analysing what else was happening at the time a text was written and first published. You can begin to find this out by using an **annals**, which functions as a short-cut summary of historical facts if you do not know much about a text's historical context. For example, Emily Bronte's novel *Wuthering Heights* was published in 1847; the annals *The Teach Yourself Encyclopedia of Dates and Events* tells us that in 1846 the term 'folk-lore' was coined (which could be relevant to the presence of fairy-tale elements in the novel).

Remember here the distinctions we drew above between causation, correlation and coincidence. Sometimes in the course of an argument a correlation or co-occurrence is incorrectly presented as a causality, e.g. by the use of 'therefore' in this sentence:

> Dickens and Thackeray were concerned with demanding social justice in an attempt to make life better, therefore their literature adopted realism as a method.

There could be a causal link between demanding social justice and realism as a method, but it is not shown. There may be merely a less direct link. It might be, for example, that the social concerns of these authors and their use of realism both come from a common source: increased knowledge of social reality as a result of sociological work in the nineteenth century and the urbanisation of Britain; that is, a correlation rather than a causation.

COMPARING TEXTS

Because a text always relates historically to other texts, one way of developing material for your essay is to compare texts. Sometimes texts are altered editorially for particular purposes, and in this respect, for example, you could compare Shakespeare's play *Macbeth* with a version of the play revised for performance in the eighteenth century. Such a comparison would tell you about changes in language and in aesthetics, about the demands of performance in the later period, and about changes in social values. Even if you have no particular interest in the play *Macbeth* itself, such a comparison helps you to learn about eighteenth-century attitudes, by providing information and insights you can then use to look at eighteenth-century drama or literature generally.

Another type of comparison arises from the fact that literary texts often adapt other sorts of text. You might compare, for instance, a real letter from 1740 with one of the letters in Richardson's novel

Pamela (published in 1740, and consisting of a sequence of imitation letters). From this you might learn about Richardson's method of writing, as well as about differences between writing that is genuinely private and writing that only pretends to be private. Or you could use a text that has been translated from one medium into another. By comparing the film *Apocalypse Now* (Francis Ford Coppola, 1979) with the story on which it is based, Joseph Conrad's *Heart of Darkness* (1902), you might gain ideas about differences between film and writing as media, or differences between an early twentieth-century text and a late twentieth-century text; you might also get ideas about narrative by comparing how far the two narratives are the same and how far they differ.

Finally, a comparison essay always involves a decision about how to organise the comparison. If for example you compare the film *Gregory's Girl* (Bill Forsyth, 1981) with Shakespeare's play *A Midsummer Night's Dream*, on which it is partly based, you could organise the comparison as:

> GG narrative compared with MND narrative; GG characterisation compared with MND characterisation; etc.; summary of comparison.

Or you could organise the comparison as:

> GG narrative, GG characterisation; MND narrative, MND characterisation; etc.; comparison between the two texts.

Generally the first mode – point-by-point argument – is preferable, since it foregrounds comparison rather than description. The second mode of presentation has the damaging tendency to defer argument and analysis until a closing section, before which come extended passages of paraphrase and basic description. Finally, remember that point-by-point comparisons can also be tedious if extended too far; formal analysis (of which close comparison is an example) always needs to be subordinated to some more general point you want to make.

BUILDING AN ARGUMENT AROUND A WORD

An argument can sometimes be built around the definition of a word. Consider for example an essay on 'Islamic elements in Byron's poetry'. One way of putting an argument together for such an essay would be to look up the word 'Romanticism' in the dictionary, since Byron's poetry belongs to this literary movement. You would probably find that there are several competing definitions, together with examples that help you think about Romanticism. On the basis of the definitions you might find you could even construct your own definition of Romanticism, and this might give direction to your essay. For example, you might define Romanticism as 'an artistic movement centrally concerned with the relationship between the self and others'. The next step would be to explore whether the 'others' in Byron's poetry might include people who follow the religion of Islam.

'Romanticism' would be a keyword for this essay. Another keyword might be 'Islamic'. Many words have a history that reflects the history of ideas and the more general history of society. One way of finding material for your essay is to look up your keyword in sources concerned with the social history of language and ideas, such as the OED or Raymond Williams' book (from which we take the term) *Keywords: A vocabulary of culture and society*. The OED for example tells you that the word 'Islam' was first used in English in a poem by Shelley, six years before Byron's death. If you now find and read that poem by Shelley, you open up the possibility of comparing Byron with Shelley in terms of how they represent Islam. The dictionary entry also suggests that the term 'Islam' was new to English-speaking culture at this time, which might prompt you to look up other words, including 'Mussulman' and 'Mohammedan'; reading the entries for these words will give you further clues relating to the representation of Islam in English-speaking cultures, and so further material for your argument.

EXERCISES

1. Choose a novel you have read, and do an experiment involving a 'flashback' structure, as follows. Read the final paragraph first, then turn to the first page and start reading. How does putting the end at the beginning change the 'feel' of the narrative? (You might try this with a novel you haven't read, which gives a better surprise effect – but potentially spoils the novel!)

2. Select a work (novel, film, play, poem, etc.) and summarise it as far as you can with a single word. Try different words as alternatives, and choose the one that best summarises the work. Now look up the word you have chosen in a dictionary, and devise some ways of using the content of the dictionary definition to organise an essay about the work. (As an alternative, or in addition, look up the word in a dictionary of quotations, and find a suitable quotation with which to begin your essay.)

WEIGHTING DIFFERENT ELEMENTS
IN YOUR ARGUMENT

In this unit, we consider how best to 'weight' elements in your argument: that is, how to present them with differing degrees of prominence, commitment and claimed significance. In particular, we show how you can distinguish between views you take for granted and views you are directly asserting.

ASSERTING, JUSTIFYING AND PRESUPPOSING

Assertion

At many points in your essay you will want to propose or just say something; many of your sentences will therefore be **assertions**. When you make an assertion, what you are doing is telling your reader something you claim is true. Assertions can be signalled as such, with varying degrees of strength or conviction, by writing 'I would suggest', or 'I would argue'. But statements without these explicit signals are also understood as assertions.

There are two important questions to be asked about any assertion you make in an essay:

1. Does the assertion need further justification?

2. Does the assertion presuppose too much?

Justification and evidence

If all your essay consisted of was a series of assertions, there would be little connection or development between its parts; there would be no argument. An assertion becomes the basis of an argument when it is combined with a **justification**. Consider the following assertion:

> Dickens showed an incorrect view of the London working classes.

Justification could be given for this assertion by describing Dickens's view of the London working classes, then describing the view of one or more modern historians, then showing that the difference between the two views allows Dickens's view to be judged incorrect. This way of arguing could be developed further by defending your assertion against an alternative, such as a Dickens critic who says that Dickens had an accurate view of these matters, and showing that this alternative view is incorrect, or at least that the critic provides insufficient supporting evidence for it. While justification of assertions is what drives your essay forward and builds your argument, however, there isn't space to justify every assertion you make; you have to judge for each case if further justification is needed.

Presupposition

When you write a sentence, you claim something is true; that is, you assert a proposition. If you write 'the second novel Dickens produced was called *Oliver Twist*', then you are asserting that it is true that the second novel Dickens produced was called Oliver Twist. As you write, however, you commit yourself not only to propositions you explicitly assert, but also to other propositions which are implicit in, or presupposed by, the words you write. In writing the above sentence, for example, you **presupposed** that Dickens produced a second novel. 'Presuppose' means that you have already supposed or claimed something without feeling a need to assert it.

Hidden commitments of this kind are often the result of using particular words, phrases or constructions, some of which we illustrate below. Consider first the following sentence:

> William Golding's best novel, *The Lord of the Flies*, is a reflection of the widespread pessimism about the morality of children in the 1950s.

This sentence makes a number of claims, some more overt than others. The overt claim is this:

> *The Lord of the Flies* is a reflection of the widespread pessimism about the morality of children in the 1950s.

But two other claims are being made as well:

> *The Lord of the Flies* is William Golding's best novel.

and

> There was widespread pessimism about the morality of children in the 1950s.

These two claims are both presupposed by the sentence; the sentence just assumes they are true. Such hidden assertions can easily be discovered. But it is less easy to notice two further presuppositions in the same sentence:

> It is possible to evaluate texts (i.e. to say that one is the 'best')

and

It is possible for texts to reflect social attitudes.

This example shows how a sentence that seems to contain one assertion can turn out to contain many different assertions, some taking the form of presuppositions. This is unavoidable; it happens all the time as you speak or write. Even so, to make your argument coherent you need to become as aware as you can of all the assertions you are making – including the hidden ones.

To help you check for presuppositions in what you write, we now provide a description of the main words, phrases and construc-tions which regularly conceal presuppositions (we have already looked at the first kind).

The
A phrase like 'the second novel Dickens produced' is not itself a statement of fact, but can be rewritten to show its presupposition ('Dickens produced a second novel'). Using the **definite article** 'the' at the beginning of a phrase implies general agreement about the existence of whatever the phrase refers to.

What is . . .

What is Kristeva's position on gender-positioning in this article?

The 'what is' construction presupposes that 'Kristeva has a position on gender-positioning in this article'.

'Again', 'once more', and other words which imply repetition

Jean Rhys began writing The Wide Sargasso Sea once more.

This presupposes that Jean Rhys had begun writing *The Wide Sargasso Sea* before.

Factive verbs like 'regret' or 'know'

Verbs like these presuppose that what is regretted or known is a fact:

> At the end of the book, the main character *regrets* believing in God.

This presupposes that 'the main character believed in God'.

Implicative verbs, which imply one action by stating another

> Romantic authors *managed* to persuade us that cities are a source of corruption.

This presupposes that Romantic writers *tried* to persuade us that cities are a source of corruption.

'Although', 'since' and 'because': connectives which conceal presuppositions

> *Because* George Orwell was a social reformer, he focused in his work on political systems.

This presupposes that George Orwell was a social reformer.

Clefts and pseudoclefts

Presuppositions can be created in a sentence simply by rearranging its parts, as in this example (called a **cleft**) based on the sentence, 'Writers such as Margaret Atwood and Angela Carter brought gender awareness into modern fiction':

> *It was* writers such as Margaret Atwood and Angela Carter *who* brought gender awareness into modern fiction.

This presupposes that *someone (or something)* brought gender aware-ness into modern fiction.

A superficially similar rearrangement (called a **pseudocleft** be-cause it looks a bit like a cleft but isn't one) is shown in this example:

> *What* contemporary novelists *do well* is comment on novel writing rather than tell stories.

This presupposes that 'contemporary novelists do *something* well.'

Counterfactual conditionals
Another sentence arrangement which carries a presupposition is the **counterfactual conditional**: 'if X had/hadn't been the case, then Y':

> *If* Harold Pinter *were* not left-wing, *The Caretaker would* be thought a far less interesting work.

This presupposes that 'Harold Pinter is left-wing.'

Context-setting clauses
Finally, presuppositions are created by kinds of clause which set the scene in a sentence, for example the italicised clause below.

> *When William Blake saw his first angels* he was sitting in his garden.

This presupposes that William Blake saw angels.

Presuppositions and hidden assumptions are a hiding place for unreflective common sense and shared assumptions. Once such assumptions are revealed, by being turned back into assertions, they often seem less easy to justify. Essentially, though, presuppositions are a tool rather than a nuisance: they allow you to imply things without saying them directly and so to develop complex arguments in relatively short passages of writing.

Given and new information

Presuppositions present ideas as **given** information; the ideas form an assumed background to what you wish to assert. Other ideas are presented as **new** information: they are what you present as being of interest. By judging which information to present as given and which to present as new, you signal to your reader what you take as common or assumed ground at any given time, and what you wish to represent as now worthy of attention.

Consider (a slightly contracted form of) one of our earlier presupposition examples:

> As a social reformer, George Orwell focused in his work on political systems.

It is presupposed here (and so given) that 'George Orwell was a social reformer'. What is presented as new is that Orwell 'focused in his work on political systems'. Now consider the two assertions arranged in reverse order:

> Focusing in his work on political systems, George Orwell was a social reformer.

Now what is presented as given information is Orwell's focus on political systems; what is presented as new is the claim that Orwell was a social reformer. Which of the two alternative means of presenting essentially the same two claims will be more appropriate depends on what you anticipate your readers will take as shared assumptions. But it also depends on what you yourself have said. If you have just shown how *Animal Farm* allegorically represents a political society and *1984* depicts an imagined, future political order, then 'focusing on political systems' is given information – because you have just given it. On the other hand, if you have just pointed to Orwell's polemical essays and his involvement in the Spanish Civil War, then the given information will be that 'Orwell was a social reformer'.

Essays, like discourse more generally, advance by initially establishing elements of information (out of presupposed material), then taking those elements as given and adding new information to them – new information that in turn becomes the given information for what follows. Much of your local editing (see Unit 11) is likely to involve re-ordering elements in sentences so that the flow of overlapping given and new information is easier to follow.

GENERALISING

So far, we have focused on specific details in your argument: facts you report and observations you make. But specific observations need to be related to broader claims, or **generalisations**. Without these, the specifics can just seem trivial and random.

Where do generalisations come from? A specific observation about some aspect of a text (e.g. its rhyme scheme) might lead to a generalisation based on how it fits with other related observations (e.g. the rhyme schemes of other poems by the same poet). A concrete comment on some special element of the text (e.g. a particularly striking metaphor) might lead to a wider, more abstract discussion of its significance beyond the text (e.g. what makes any metaphor striking?). Generalising from your experience of reading a passage or from a specific observation you have made leads into speculation about regularities and patterns.

Generalisations encourage you to think about causation and correlation, which are central to explanation and argument (see Unit 8). They are important as a means of obliging you to go beyond describing the details of your individual experience as a reader, and enabling you to make statements about literary patterns or structures of interest to other people.

Two kinds of generalisation in literary studies are especially common.

- You broaden points you are making, so that they apply to other books, or to an author's work as a whole.

> *Example*: In an essay on a play which presents women characters as generally a source of disruption or confusion, you conclude by asking whether, in drama of the particular period or style, women are generally presented as sources of disruption.

- You treat a specific question or topic as an instance of a more general question or topic.

> *Example*: the topic 'Islamic elements in Byron's poetry' is given greater interest and significance by placing it in a more general discussion of 'foreignness' in British Romantic texts.

GIVING EXAMPLES

Generalisations are created when specific observations accumulate into or prompt broader statements. Working outwards from observation into generalisation is likely to be the order in which things happen as you research and write. But once you have your generalisations, it is often better to present them the other way round: you make a general claim or argument (an explanation of something, or a claim about patterning or structure), then you illustrate that claim with examples which function as the evidence for the claim.

Throughout any argument you need to provide examples of general categories; but at some specific points in your argument you will need to illustrate links you are making between your categories as well. Consider our Orwell example again: 'As a social reformer,

George Orwell focused in his work on political systems'. The category 'social reformer' is a generalisation, and can be exemplified by for example suggesting that Orwell's polemical essays and involvement in the Spanish Civil War demonstrate a wish to bring about social change. You can also exemplify the general category 'focus in his work on political systems' by showing how *Animal Farm* represents a political society rather than a farm, and how *1984* depicts an imagined, future political order. More challenging is to find an example of the generalised link you claim (because you presupposed it) between the two ideas: what connects social reformers in general with concern in their work with political systems? Here your examples will not be from Orwell, but rather of other writers whose engagement with political systems in their writing has been viewed as contributing to social change.

Achieving a balance between specific examples and general claims, and linking the two together so that the examples function effectively as evidence for the claims, is a major editing task. Too many examples, or links that are too weak between examples and general claims, and the essay will not make a convincing argument. Too few specific examples, or examples which are not tied closely enough to general claims to act as evidence for them, and the essay will read as merely a series of impressions, opinions or even prejudices.

SIGNALLING ATTITUDE TO YOUR OWN ARGUMENT

As you construct your argument, the particular forms in which you present material express judgements about how firmly you are committed to each of your argument's component ideas, and how strong the evidence is for believing them. An unqualified assertion, as we saw above, states something you take to be true. Qualifying the same assertion by writing 'I would suggest', or 'I would argue' enables you to signal varying degrees of strength or conviction you are giving that assertion. This way of qualifying an assertion is one of a number of strategies for showing where you stand in relation to the substance of what you write.

Epistemic modality

Throughout your essay, you face the question of how firm your evidence is for believing something: Do you know it? Believe that it is almost certainly true? Think it likely? Consider it a possibility? Such issues are matters of **epistemic modality** (the word 'epistemic' means 'to do with knowledge'). Epistemic modality involves various markers in language of the degree of certainty or possibility a speaker or writer feels towards what is being said. It includes modal verbs such as 'must' and 'may', as well as phrases such as 'it is possible that . . .', 'it is likely that . . .'. A range of adverbial expressions, including 'apparently' and 'actually', have a similar effect.

Two different kinds of problematic situation are likely to arise as you present your argument. The first is that what you say seems obvious; so, in slight embarrassment, you add 'obviously' or 'of course' – implying 'of course everyone knows this'. The second situation is that you feel there is a risk of overstating the line of argument you are pursuing.

Consider first the effect of adding 'of course' to a sentence.

Dickens of course believed that . . .

If we already know what we are being told – as 'of course' implies – then why are we being told again? Sometimes, by contrast, 'of course' is added not because the information is obvious, but rather because the writer wishes to create the effect of being someone so deeply familiar with the material that this information is basic or obvious, though only to such a person. Consider the different impression of yourself – and of your expectations about readers – created by writing one or other of the sentences below.

Dickens, of course, was a novelist.

vs

Dickens, of course, completed the last double instalment of *Martin Chuzzlewit* in the middle of June 1844.

There is no fixed rule governing use of 'of course'. What you need to do is to anticipate what effect your use of this expression is likely to have, on a given occasion, on your probable readers – and act accordingly.

Hedges

The other type of difficult situation arises when a claim you are making looks overstated (possibly unsustainable in its generalised form, or stronger than the evidence you have properly warrants). In these circumstances, you tone down what you are saying by using indicators (called **hedges**) that show you recognise the difficulty of certainty in the area in question.

To use a hedge, you modify simple statements of fact or opinion with a phrase such as 'it seems likely that . . .', 'this may be . . .', 'it is reasonable to suppose that . . .', or occasionally with 'relatively', 'in effect', 'seemingly' or 'it seems that'. Other useful words here are 'evidently', 'rather', 'somewhat', 'generally', 'on the whole', 'can appear to', and 'arguably'. Take special care with 'arguably', however. This word works well as a hedge in respect of a passing topic (e.g. 'this is arguably also the case in works by Jeanette Winterson other than *Oranges Are Not The Only Fruit* . . .'). But if you use 'arguably' in respect of a central or major argument you are making, you invite the unspoken response: 'Well, if it's arguable, then let's *hear* the arguments, since this is what the essay is supposed to be about.'

In using hedging and qualifying expressions, you should note that they may affect the overall impression your essay creates. They may, for example, suggest that you have no confidence in your argument or even that you are incapable of making up your mind. In general it is safe to assume that your reader will bring to your work an overall expectation that you will be saying things you cannot be sure of but that, as you say those things, you will be making your best effort to demonstrate their truth. For this reason, most hedges are best removed.

EXERCISE

Consider this introduction to an essay:

> Shakespeare's birth in 1564 marks the beginning of the high period of English drama. When he later produced a series of outstanding tragic works, what he managed to do, in effect, was to bring about the transition from crude Medieval drama towards the more sustained literary achievement of the Renaissance.

List all the presuppositions you think the passage contains. Now asterisk those you think would need justification in an essay called 'Shakespeare's influence on modern tragedy', leaving others which you feel can stand without support. Look more closely now at the presuppositions you *haven't* asterisked: why don't these presuppositions need justification or explanation in the way the others do? Finally, use our discussion of epistemic modals and hedges above to decide how you might present points you feel need justification but which you don't have full evidence for.

THE VOICE TO WRITE IN

In this unit, we consider how you develop an appropriate voice to write in, since this is how you convey a sense of yourself as the writer of your essay. Your 'voice' is achieved in two main ways, and we discuss each in turn: by means of a particular style you adopt, and in the relationship you establish between yourself and the reader. After outlining the main features of a conventionally appropriate style for essays in literary studies, we show how essay style creates meanings and effects – including effects it is better to avoid.

YOUR REGISTER AND YOUR VOICE

In different situations we write and speak differently. The difference is one of **register**, a technical term which describes a variety of language which is distinctively used in a specific context. For example, a birthday card greeting is written in a different register from a legal contract; it uses a different vocabulary, different layout on the page, uses rhyme, etc.

To see that this is the case, annotate each term below to say whether it belongs to the typical register of the birthday card or the register of the legal contract. Even if you've never seen a legal contract you can probably do this.

vocabulary:	henceforth • you're
punctuation:	! :
layout:	two words on a line • rhyme • numbered pages
typeface:	small print • big print

Our choice of register contributes to the **voice** we write in ('writing voice' here alludes to the notion of speaking voice, in which we express attitude by intonation, tempo and other means). Imagine the consequences of writing a birthday card in the register of a legal contract (and vice versa).

The academic essay or dissertation is a 'situation' that has its own appropriate register, a register that should be used consistently throughout. Creating that register involves making a compromise between an anonymous, generic 'essay voice' and your own personal voice. The 'anonymous' element is a voice that should be fairly formal, and evidently a written register rather than a written-down version of how you speak. The 'personal' element comes from avoiding terminology or phrasing with which you are uncomfortable, or which you would only use to imitate someone else's writing: over-formality is also a fault. To find the appropriate voice for you, try saying your sentences aloud. They should sound like written sentences read aloud, but they should still sound like *your* sentences. This basic rule can be broken for deliberate effect. But, as always in writing, it is your understanding of the underlying conventions that will allow you to judge when to break them and when not to.

Academic register is not your spoken voice

Table 2, below, shows some of the features of the register of conversational speech that an academic essay register avoids.

In this book we do use (i) contractions and (ii) emphatic uses. This is because the book is a textbook of a certain kind; the contractions are intended to create a relaxed and informal tone, while

Table 2 Academic vs conversational register

Avoid	Replace with
(i) Contractions like *there's, it's, they've*, etc.	The full words: *there is, it is, they have*, etc.
(ii) Emphatic use of italics, capitals or underlining	If you have to be emphatic, do it in words such as *I wish to emphasise that...*
(iii) Exclamations, including exclamation marks: *What a bad poem this is!*	If you need to express a strong opinion say for example *In my view this is not a good poem*
(iv) Colloquialisms: *naff, O.K., maybe*	Replace with more formal words with similar meanings: *unsuccessful, acceptable, perhaps*

the emphatic uses reflect encouragement to see some points we are making as being in contrast to what is generally assumed. Your essay is not a textbook and should not adopt the specific register features of textbooks, either this one or others.

Standardisation

Essay-writing involves a standardised, written variety of language. The fact that the variety is standardised can be problematic as regards any suggestion that your essay voice will be an adapted version of your own voice. Varieties of language which depend on the location of the speaker are called **dialects**, and switching from dialect forms into a standardised voice involves political questions of identity as well as narrowly linguistic decisions. Many dialects, when written, are not accepted as standardised forms. For example in spoken Glasgow dialect a sentence can end with adverbial 'but', but while this can be written down as a sentence ending in 'but', it will not be generally accepted as satisfying the requirements of academic register. There is no good reason for this, other than convention. On the other hand, Scottish English does have words, such as 'out-with' (meaning 'beyond' or 'except for'), which are specific to the dialect and are also acceptable in formal academic register.

Sentence length and sentence complexity

Written sentences are often longer than spoken sentences, and can use punctuation as a way of indicating structure; so they can cope more easily with the grammatical complexity of sentences containing sub-sentences or sub-clauses. Despite this capability, formal written registers nevertheless still often favour relatively short sentences, which help keep writing clear and understandable. But if very short, simple sentences dominate your writing, it will inevitably become monotonous. So you should keep in mind the possibility of building more complex thoughts by building more complex sentences.

Consider this extract, which involves a sequence of short sentences (we have added numbers to make the sentences easier to identify):

(1) Both Bronte and Hardy choose to present their heroine within an organic structure. (2) This reflects their development. (3) Themes of nature and setting are apparent in both novels. (4) They are used in relation to the heroines' development in various ways.

To create greater stylistic variation and interest, we could rewrite the extract by combining sentences (1) and (2), and sentences (3) and (4):

As a way of reflecting the development of their heroines, both Bronte and Hardy present their heroines within an organic structure. Themes of nature and setting, which are used in relation to the heroines' development in various ways, are apparent in both novels.

It would have been equally possible to combine the sentences using semi-colons (which are usually interchangeable with full stops, see Unit 14). The full stop between the two sentences of our rewritten version would be replaced by a semi-colon, so turning the original four short sentences into a single, more complex sentence. But you do come to a limit with long sentences. More than about four lines for a single sentence places unreasonable demands on your reader.

Agency and passives

In some academic styles, particularly in the reporting of scientific experiments, **passive sentences** are commonly preferred to active sentences. A passive sentence is a sentence in which the agent of an action is either not mentioned (as in the first example below), or is de-emphasised by being placed later in the sentence (as in the second example below).

> The Yellow Book and the Decadents were always seen to be associated with Oscar Wilde.

> The evolution of the novel is transformed by Jane Austen.

Passives should be used carefully. Literary studies is not scientific experimentation; we are interested in particular people and their agency as much as in general properties and processes, and especially interested in the agency of an author. So it is appropriate to move people more up front, as in the following non-passive ('active') sentence:

> Jane Austen transforms the evolution of the novel.

And if we are interested in agency, then we should take some responsibility for attributing it; so in the 'Oscar Wilde' example above we should also say who it was that saw this association.

Parentheticals

A **parenthetical** is a sentence in brackets or separated by dashes, inserted into another sentence. Such sentences are like footnotes inserted into the text, and the same general principle normally applies: if they are important, don't leave them in parenthesis, and if they are unimportant, delete them. Parentheticals also make a sentence longer, while keeping the grammatical structure chosen for a shorter sentence; this can make such sentences difficult to read. Try taking the content of your parenthetical and rewriting it as a separate, non-parenthetical sentence.

Rhetorical questions

A **rhetorical question** is a question you ask in order to create an effect. You don't expect an answer; instead you offer one yourself. Rhetorical questions can be a good way of signalling the **dialogic** nature of your writing (i.e. that it is 'like a dialogue'): they show that you are engaging with your reader, by anticipating responses and questions as you go along.

But rhetorical questions can be over-used, especially where answers to the questions do not follow immediately. Consider this rhetorical question, from an essay on *Othello*:

> Does this tell us about Shakespeare? Is he guilty of racial discrimination?

If the essay now abandons these questions and introduces another topic, then the questions have not engaged with the reader but rather suspended debate, after having introduced, tantalisingly, an area for speculation. In this case, the essay goes on,

> The aim is not to apportion blame but to uncover the origins of racial stereotyping and how they have permeated English Literature.

The general issue of 'racial discrimination' is picked up here, in the idea of 'racial stereotyping'; but the specific issue of Shakespeare's guilt is not – it has been raised but not dealt with. Rhetorical questions work, then, when they are answered in what follows, and so long as they are not over-used.

MODE OF ADDRESS

Many of the choices you make in creating your essay register relate to your subject matter. But others serve to create a relationship between you and your reader. The means by which you establish this relationship are often called the interpersonal dimension of register: the **mode of address** you adopt. The main choices you make in this respect concern how you refer to yourself as the writer, who you think your reader is, and how you address that reader.

Referring to yourself

When referring to yourself as the writer of your essay, it is possible to use a range of forms: 'I', 'we', 'one', 'the present author', etc. Traditionally, however, there are restrictions on straightforwardly saying 'I'. Some teachers forbid it outright, as an example of inelegant intrusion by the author. Mostly nowadays, though, it is considered permissible occasionally (e.g. to emphasise a point you wish to show is personal rather than general). The guiding principle must be this: that the overall interest of your essay lies in how well its combination of observation and argument leads to more general statements, and so away from the particularity of autobiography and personal impression. Too much use of 'I' (especially, 'I think', 'I noticed', 'I much prefer', etc.) will hold the essay back from achieving a suitable level of generalisation.

Here are some ways to get round the need to refer to yourself (you can vary them to avoid any over-formulaic effect).

- Adverbs and adverbial expressions: replace 'I think it is likely that . . .' with 'Arguably, . . .'.
- Passives: rewrite 'I argue below that . . .' as 'it is argued below that . . .'.

- Personification of your essay itself as an agent: rewrite 'in this essay I explain how' as 'this essay explains how . . .'.

Bear in mind, though, as you weigh up these alternatives, what we have said about passives and personification in our discussion above, and about 'arguably' in our discussion of hedges in Unit 9.

'One' and 'we' in particular should be avoided as ways of referring to yourself. They now seem **archaic** (old fashioned) and pompous, especially if embedded in a more colloquial register. Authorial 'we' (e.g. 'we will argue below') should also be avoided. Apart from allowing in traditionally disliked personal comment, both 'one' and 'we' produce an effect of generalised response: 'one' combines the personal dimension of 'I' with the general character-istic of 'anyone' (i.e. the writer serves as a norm or representative of everyone else); and 'we' (at least in its inclusive use as readers, 'we feel in this passage', rather than as authorial 'we, the author') suggests generalised reader-reaction. The idea that any reader will respond as you do is something you may not wish to convey, espe-cially if you intend your essay to show openness to the possibility of different readings being produced by different sorts of reader or on different occasions.

The precise degree to which you decide to use techniques for avoiding 'I' and 'we' will depend on the overall register you are trying to produce. But you should certainly avoid obvious personal intrusions, such as the two following:

- The confession

  > Sorry, I had no time to complete this essay, so I have made some basic points that I would have brought out and discussed.

- The embedded 'letter' (a direct address to the reader, sometimes with apology or denunciation of the course)

  > Isn't there a problem with the way you have formulated this question? I should have thought that . . .

Addressing the reader

Second person pronouns are not generally accepted in academic writing any more than first person ones. This characteristic of the idiom is linked to the notion that criticism is less concerned with any one particular reader than with an unspecified general reader-ship. This view of a readership is often, as we suggested in Unit 4, deeply at odds with the actual circumstances of essay-writing in literature courses. But it remains a conventional feature of academic style, and your writing will produce very marked effects if you deviate from this convention.

Ways round using 'you' overlap with the ways of avoiding 'I' and 'we'. For example, you can replace 'in this essay I will tell you' with 'this essay explains how . . .', and 'you might see this phrase as meaning . . .' with something like 'this phrase may be interpreted as meaning . . .'.

Take special care with (sometimes indirect) forms of address to your reader that signal an attitude you may not wish to suggest. In the following example, an indirect instruction to the reader to give particular attention to a point conveys an unfortunate condescend-ing attitude:

> The reader would do well to consider this point carefully.

Referring to the reader in the third person

Our last example shows how you can address your reader indirectly, by referring in the third person to 'the reader', where 'the reader' means 'you'. But when you write a sentence of this kind, you do not know whether your reader is male or female. So a choice is needed if the sentence is to continue:

> The reader would do well to consider this point carefully if he is to grasp the poet's intentions fully.

This writer has chosen to use 'he' as a **generic** to mean 'male or female', overriding the normal use of 'he' as a gender-specific pronoun meaning 'male'. While this used to be common practice, it is now widely considered sexist: such usage represents the masculine as the norm, and so marginalises women. In the case of this link between 'reader . . . he', the 'male as norm' terminology creates the impression that educated discussion of literature takes place only among men (even though literary study was established in Britain in the nineteenth century as a subject largely for women, and now has a significant majority of women involved in it).

There are various alternatives to traditional, 'generic' usage. Both male and female pronouns can be used:

> . . . if he or she is to grasp the poet's intentions fully.

But there is no particular reason to put 'he' first, so you could just as easily write:

> . . . if she or he is to grasp the poet's intentions fully.

Or you can rewrite the sentence so that the plural pronoun is used:

> Readers would do well to consider this point carefully if they are to grasp the poet's intentions fully.

Or you can use 's/he', replacing 'he and/or she'. Or you can use 'she' *as a generic*, directly challenging the older use of 'he':

> . . . if she is to grasp the poet's intentions fully.

You might argue that in each of these cases the need to choose arises only because the reader is addressed obliquely in the third person, rather than being directly addressed as 'you'. This is true, but rewording would not make difficulties presented by generic and gendered pronouns disappear: you will in any case need to choose suitable pronoun forms in other contexts in your essay. You can avoid addressing your reader indirectly as 'the reader'; but you will almost certainly refer to the reader of the works you are discussing rather than the reader of your own essay – and then you will face exactly the same set of issues when you need to refer back to that reader.

REACTING TO VOICES OUTSIDE YOUR ADOPTED REGISTER

Most of your writing in an academic register involves working to achieve a voice that is partly conventional and partly personal, but as far as possible consistent. Consider this extract from an essay on the poem 'Marriage' by Marianne Moore as an example of register not being achieved consistently:

> Moore states her case combining wit and sharp, almost black, humour in attempting to ridicule male vanity in marital union. Marriage is seen as despicable through the force and longevity of the poem. However, she still retains a trademark in the numerous quotes and sources of thought she incorporates into the text, providing ammunition from scholarly sources in proving her point, even if it means twisting what they say to fit her point of view.

Notice here the phrase 'marital union' in the first sentence. This is no doubt used partly to avoid repeating 'marriage', which is the title of the poem and so has already been used more than once. But the phrase used instead ('marital union') introduces another (religious or moral?) register that clashes with the rest of the paragraph. Consider, too, the word 'longevity' in the next sentence. It is difficult to make sense of this word here (since 'longevity' means 'length of life', rather than simply 'length', and is difficult to apply, except metaphorically, to a poem). The effort that has been made to find a technical or elevated alternative to 'length' results here only in a comic effect (a sort of **malapropism**, or effect of trying to use

words which are not fully understood). Finally, consider the word
'quotes' in the third sentence, or the common metaphorical senses
of 'trademark' (meaning 'a distinctive feature or characteristic'), or
'ammunition' (meaning 'some powerful means of support'). These
words introduce an element of informality – especially 'quotes',
which is a marked alternative to 'quotations' – that pulls the
paragraph in exactly the opposite direction from the upward shift in
register attempted in 'marital union'. The resulting tension makes
the register of the paragraph overall slightly comical, largely because
it is inconsistent.

Stylistic imitation

One common cause of register inconsistency in essays is imitation
of the voices of other writers, a tendency that is also common in
published literary criticism. During the 1950s and 1960s, for example, the vocabulary and style of the influential critic F.R. Leavis
were imitated extensively (e.g. in use of such words as 'equipoise'
and 'maturity' to describe writers' qualities, or phrases such as 'it
seems to me that . . .'). Imitation can be a way of showing you
belong to a tradition or 'school' of criticism, whose influence
extends into influence on style as well as on ideas, beliefs or theories.
In fact, the two overlap, when certain key words are understood in
senses that presume familiarity with how they have been used
previously. One example of this is the term 'Orientalism', which has
shifted from an earlier, favourable or neutral sense into a specialised,
polemical meaning, following discussion of the term in Edward
Said's book *Orientalism*. Choosing to imitate a register can also
reflect beliefs about the purpose of literary analysis (e.g. is it a form
of humanistic debate, in which case conventions of gentle persuasion should be observed; or is it investigative research, in which case
more rigorous and systematic discourse is required?).

   If you do decide to imitate a critical voice or style – something
which is usually inappropriate in assessed essays – you still need to be
consistent as far as possible. Moments of departing from the imitated
style will produce kinds of incongruity similar to those in the
Marianne Moore example above.

Stylistic infection

In some essays, rather than imitating a critical style, the style in which the essay is written 'catches' characteristics of the material the essay is about. The result is poetic essays about poems; ironic essays about ironic texts; satirical essays about satire, etc. Often this effect on essay style comes from enthusiasm on the part of the essay writer for the style of the passage being discussed. But one consequence of such stylistic infection is that it reduces the difference between the text being written about and the essay itself, and dissolves the boundary (and difference of purpose) between the two. There are things to be said about irony that it may not be possible to say ironically; an ironic essay on irony will fail to address such issues. In examinations, stylistic infection can be a particular problem, in that it is likely such writing will not answer the prescribed question very closely. Note, too, that if you write ironically you run the risk of appearing to satirise the question, or the process of analytical writing about literature more generally.

INCORPORATING EXPRESSIONS FROM OUTSIDE YOUR ADOPTED REGISTER

There are several situations, however, in which you will actively wish to incorporate expressions that do not easily fit into your adopted voice. Quotations, for example, bring with them the register of their original source, though they do not generally present problems because they are clearly marked off from your own voice by conventions of presentation (conventions we discuss in Unit 13). Here we consider two other instances where boundaries between your own voice and other idioms are less clear, and need to be established.

Technical terms

Technical terms are a characteristic of academic essay register, but how far you use them will depend on which 'school' of literary criticism you align yourself with. Technical terms present two problems. First they may need to be signalled as technical terms, because a word may have a technical and a non-technical meaning ('story', 'discourse', 'theory' are all like this). To indicate technical terms, you might put them in inverted commas or capitalise the first letter of the word. Don't, however, put the whole word in capitals, italics or boldface; this is specific to textbook register. The second, more difficult problem is that of ensuring that your reader understands what your technical terms mean, or (more usually in an assessed essay) letting your reader know that *you* know what they mean. You could add a **gloss** (i.e. an explanation or paraphrase), as in the following example (the gloss is italicised):

> In these lines of the poem, the 'structural parallelism', *or equivalence of grammatical structure between the two phrases,* makes us consider the two phrases synonymous.

Such glosses can embed technical terms effectively even in a register which is in other respects informal. When you first introduce a technical term that needs explanation, either gloss it immediately or indicate that you will explain it shortly. Your reader will then know that you are not presuming she knows what the term means.

Glosses should not become obtrusive, however. You need to decide which terms to gloss; some terms will have conventional meanings in the genre you are writing in, while other terms – like 'synonymous' in the above quotation – will also be common in non-technical discourse. If in doubt, you can get help with deciding whether to explain a term by consulting a dictionary of critical terms, to see which terms other people – the dictionary's editor for example – have decided merit explanation.

Other people's terms

When introduced for the first time, technical terms are helpfully identified by having inverted commas round them. This shows that they are words you are mentioning, or borrowing from another type of discourse, rather than words you are using in your own voice. Another, contrasting function served by inverted commas (besides direct quotation) is that of distancing you from an expression. Sometimes this is desirable because the expression seems awkward or inadequate; sometimes it signals that the expression does not fit with the rest of the register you have adopted.

Such inverted commas are often called **scare quotes**, and are used especially in philosophically-inspired criticism which is sceptical about the customary senses we give to words. Technically, by putting a word in scare quotes you are **mentioning** the word rather than **using** it, holding it up for critical examination rather than saying it yourself. Scare quotes sound the alarm, alerting readers to the idea that something is deficient or inappropriate about the word being used.

Take care, however. While it is valuable to show your awareness of complexities in the words we use to conceptualise things, scare quotes may not be the best way of showing this. In some cases, consulting a thesaurus will offer an alternative. In other cases, explicit discussion of the difficulties presented by the expression is more helpful, if this does not distract too much from the progression of your argument. Remember that scare quotes are simply disclaimers ('this isn't my word, so don't blame me for its implications'); they don't solve – or even identify – the problems that the word presents. At worst, they merely signal a reluctance or inability to grapple with those problems. Philosophically, it could in any case be argued that most or all words present analogous difficulties, and need to be put in scare quotes ('the "topic" of this "essay" is the "issue" of the "author's" "intentions"', etc.). So if you start using scare quotes, it may be the words you don't put them round which become the problem.

EXPRESSING TASTE AND VALUE

To conclude, we consider one particular moment in writing an essay in literary studies that creates special register difficulties: representing your own feelings or responses. Many conventional, literary-critical terms for representing feeling can sound dated, affected, or even a parody of reviewing or criticism: 'forceful', 'affecting', or 'tellingly apt'. Other expressions seem as if they may be intended ironically, and used to mean something different from the praise they appear to give: 'interesting', 'original', or 'thought-provoking'.

Such effects can be difficult to avoid, even if you follow established conventions. In literary criticism, for example, statements of praise are conventionally handled in a low-key way, often by slipping in a word that indicates skill, like the italicised adjectives and adverbs in these examples:

> In *Possession*, A.S. Byatt is *careful* not to represent romance as . . .
> Toni Morrison *deftly* handles the issue of . . .
> The second stanza *subtly* introduces the theme of . . .

These words convey critical approval. But even when conventionally handled, such expressions can introduce meanings you may not intend as well as a slight oddity of register. The first example, for instance, implies that A.S. Byatt took special care not to represent romance in a particular way, even though we have no basis for saying what was going on in her head. In any case, many literary theories deny the possibility of talking about intention; so you should be careful – especially if your essay assumes one of these theories – not to let your language make claims you don't intend. The third example above ('The second stanza . . .') suggests that the poem is being subtle, whereas in fact it is the author – with again the problem of unknowable intention. Personifying also involves a minor lapse in logic which you should be aware of, even if you decide that the final effect is worth it.

Less favourable comments about writers require equal care. Do not, for instance, appear to patronise or condescend to the writer (e.g. 'Keats is to be congratulated for his use of rhyme . . .'). Pointing out limitations can seem arrogant, as in this extract:

> At times Eliot is too confusing, too abstract and too well read, but his poems initially only demand a first response or simply an appreciation of the words, their structure, sound and order. Eliot uses at times a simplistic traditional form which incorporates elements of modernism, i.e. the subject matter providing a quirky pattern common in some poems.

Notice the effect produced here by the repeated word 'too', which suggests a slightly dismissive superiority on the part of the writer – an effect reinforced by the words 'simplistic' and 'quirky'.

In contrast with conventional literary-critical vocabulary, you may prefer terms taken from seemingly more immediate, informal speech. But words and phrases such as 'brilliant', 'fantastic', 'really wonderful', 'quite magical', or 'unbelievably beautiful' will make your register too informal. Apart from their informality, in fact, these terms will create a further difficulty, because of their tendency towards apparent exaggeration or overstatement of feeling – a difficulty that can arise even in the more conventionally acceptable register of the following example:

> There are many concerns that make the book very interesting indeed.

By surrounding the adjective 'interesting' here with two intensifiers – 'very' and 'indeed' – the writer seems to recognise that the word 'interesting' itself is somehow inadequate as an expression of feeling. In such circumstances, though, it is better to choose a different adjective (or more extended description), and dispense with the 'very' and the 'indeed'.

EXERCISE

The following passage contains a number of register inconsistencies. Using our discussion in this unit, edit it so that it conforms more to what you now understand to be conventions of an appropriate literary-critical style. (Try to alter the sense of the passage as little as possible while making your revisions.)

There is dichotomy in the defiance of moral law in Marlowe's *Edward II*. For at the play's inception Edward is berated by Mortimer and the other earls for his base acts with Gaveston; and in defiance of well defined laws of divine right and birthright Mortimer attempts to depose a crowned king. Both acts are morally wrong – Edward should not have abused his divine right and curried favour by dishing out peerages. Conversely Mortimer should not have invoked the earls to revolt against the king. So at the nub of Marlowe's play is the morality of deposition and the morality of a married king shunning his wife in favour of a homosexual lover.

REVISING AN ESSAY DRAFT

In this unit, we consider editing at different levels of essay organisation. First we explain why your essays should always be divided into paragraphs and sometimes also into sections; and we show how to manage these two means of indicating structure. We then consider how connectives and other forms of sign-posting signal relationships between steps in your argument. We conclude by offering some practical suggestions about how to implement editing decisions using word-processing tools.

SHOWING YOUR ESSAY'S STRUCTURE

In Unit 7 we discussed how an outline helps you see what needs to go where in your essay. Using the outline, you can divide the essay into sections of text corresponding to sections in the outline, and give those sections headings. String those headings together to see how far you can understand what the essay will say without referring to any other material; inconsistencies, contradictions, repetition or unexpected jumps as you link together the headings in your mind indicates that further work is needed on the essay's structure.

A similar test can be applied to paragraphs. But whereas sections commonly have titles, the main point or direction of a paragraph is usually indicated in its opening sentence, which is sometimes called a **topic sentence**. Instead of linking section headings together to test for structure, therefore, at paragraph level you need to read through a text by reading only the first sentence of each paragraph. Try this with a published essay to see how much work of summary and sign-posting is done by the topic sentences.

Shifting between 'levels' of argument in this way – upwards and downwards between any given sentence, the topic sentence of the paragraph it is in, the relevant section title, and your outline structure – clarifies what purpose any given sentence you are writing or rewriting needs to serve in terms of the essay as a whole. Indicating structure clearly at several levels strengthens your final essay. It is also a way of making it easier to write. Only as the essay approaches completion should you consider removing structure markers, since too many in the final version may make some essays seem all scaffolding, no building. To make the structure less explicit, delete paragraph headings, and possibly remove numbered or titled section headings if the essay is short.

Sections

One major reason for breaking your essay into parts is to signal how each part relates to the whole. Sections should show the logical or rhetorical relationship between them: e.g. cause and effect; particu-larisation and specification (going into greater detail); illustration (but if so, exemplifying what exactly?). If you use sub-sections, you can also reflect the relationship between parts of your argument by numbering them (1, 1.1, 1.2, etc.); the numbering indicates hierarchical relationships – a sort of family tree – between topics. Titles should indicate what sections contain, so avoid formal names like 'Introduction' and 'Conclusion' that apply to any essay and are largely redundant. Instead say something like 'Introduction: symbol-ism as an issue in Maya Angelou's writing', or 'Conclusion: the future of Reader Response approaches'.

Paragraphs

A short essay covering four A4 pages (about 1,500 words) might well be divided into about ten paragraphs. Too few paragraphs will make the essay difficult to follow, both visually and conceptually, and may suggest that it lacks any underlying argument structure. If the paragraphs are consistently very short, on the other hand (e.g. just one or two sentences), then the sub-divisions they create become too complicated for a more general structure to be deduced; this defeats the point of having paragraphs at all. Typically a paragraph will have several sentences and might number 150–200 words, covering about half a page of A4. Only very exceptionally will a paragraph consist of a single sentence, and you should never write a series of single-sentence paragraphs.

The number of paragraphs, however, is less important than the function they serve. Paragraphing takes the essay's structure to the next level down from section level, in that each paragraph relates what comes next both to the last point you have made and to the structure of the essay as a whole.

Consider how a paragraph is structured in slightly more detail. We have said that in English each paragraph is typically unified by the fact that it brings together material around a single point or topic indicated in the first sentence. One way of achieving this is to structure your paragraph as follows.

- *First sentence*: topic sentence, which makes the main claim of the paragraph and also tries to link the paragraph with what came before.
- *Subsequent sentences*: these justify or illustrate the claim.
- *Final sentence*: this sentence sums up the paragraph, and perhaps also links the paragraph with what comes next.

This basic pattern is illustrated by the following four-sentence paragraph (here split into parts and with sentence numbers added):

- topic sentence makes the main claim of the paragraph

(1) In Chapter Two Fitzgerald introduces one of the most important patterns of the novel: the 'waste land motif'.

- subsequent sentences justify or illustrate the claim

> (2) Nothing in the book emphasises the corruption of
> the American dream more than this image of 'the valley
> of ashes'. (3) In 1922 T.S. Eliot published his highly
> influential poem, 'The Waste Land', in which he described
> Western civilisation in terms of decay and desperation.

- final sentence sums up the paragraph

> (4) In The Great Gatsby Fitzgerald picks up the theme:
> the valley of ashes is the general locale, all the characters
> of the story have to pass through it.

In this example, sentence (1) introduces the topic of the paragraph:
the functioning of the 'waste land motif' in the organisation of *The
Great Gatsby*. Sentence (2) then offers a meaning for the motif: a
critique of the corruption of the American dream. Sentence (3)
opens with an apparent change of topic; but it implicitly connects
that new topic with the already-established topic of the paragraph in
a thematic parallel – to be found in T.S. Eliot's concern with 'decay
and desperation' – that also provides the name of the motif, the
'waste land motif'. Finally, in sentence (4) the parallel between Eliot
and Fitzgerald is drawn explicitly: how the motif works in the novel
is explained, so completing a miniature demonstration of what was
promised at the beginning in the paragraph's topic sentence.

As well as having internal structure, the various paragraphs that
make up an essay are linked together so that each paragraph relates
what will come next to the last point you have made. Connections
between paragraphs tend not to be made explicitly (e.g. by means
of statements such as 'in the last paragraph, I have argued . . .');
rather, they are signalled by showing that points you have just made
in the argument will now be taken as given information. This is
typically achieved by means of phrases such as 'this X', or 'the idea

that X', where X is a term or phrase introduced in the previous paragraph.

SIGN-POSTING AND CONNECTIVES

Most sentences in written prose are explicitly linked to the sentence that precedes them, producing an overall effect of **cohesion**; and as we have just seen this is the case between paragraphs as well as within them. Continuous discourse builds on what has just been said by using a combination of repeated elements ('this X', as above), omission of some things that will be inferred and therefore don't need to be said again, and specialised linking devices usually called **connectives**.

Consider this brief passage (numbers have been added to identify sentences):

> (1) One of the functions of a literary work is to pass on some crucial truths or information, give some didactic indications, or convince the reader of some general laws. (2) The dream vision convention was employed by the Middle English writers for such reasons; (3) and it enjoyed great popularity. (4) Discovering this literary phenomenon, we should realise that the contemporary reader of Middle English lived in a different social and cultural reality from ours. (5) So the dream vision must have had a tremendous impact on his perception of the world.

This paragraph is held together by the same sort of unity, or development of ideas, that we described in the *Great Gatsby* example above. But we can also identify here a series of formal markers of connection between sentences. Sentence (2) is connected to (1), for instance, by the phrase 'for such reasons', which refers back to the reasons listed in (1). It is also connected back to (1) by the fact that the 'dream vision convention' is recognisable as an aspect of 'a literary work' referred to in (1). Sentence (3) is linked to sentence (2) by the additive connective 'and', as well as by the fact that 'it' refers back to 'dream vision convention'. (4) is connected with (3) by the word 'this', which again refers to 'dream vision convention', as well as by the repetition of 'Middle English'. (5) connects with (4) because of a number of features: the repetition of 'dream vision'; the logical connection indicated by 'so'; the connection in meaning between 'world' and the phrase 'social and cultural reality'; and by the fact that 'his' refers back to the 'contemporary reader'.

Formal markers of connection achieve two related effects in academic writing (as in discourse more generally). Firstly, they bind your writing together as a single entity, providing a connectedness that makes your writing read as a whole rather than as a string of separate jottings. Secondly, many of the markers signal specific – often logical – relationships between one sentence and another (as 'so' does in the passage above); such markers control the progression of your writing from idea to idea. For this reason, it is important in essay writing to learn how to handle markers of cohesion, and to sensitise yourself to the underlying relations of meaning they signal.

Table 3 lists some of the main underlying meaning relations (with examples of common expressions used to indicate each type of relation).

As you edit, you can test your essay's cohesion by underlining its cohesive devices and seeing, for example, how your pattern of

Table 3 Underlying meaning relations with examples

Underlying meaning relation	Common expressions
Consequence	*accordingly, as a result, hence, therefore, thus*
Likeness	*analogously, correspondingly, similarly*
Contrast	*but, however, nevertheless, on the contrary, on the other hand, yet*
Exemplification	*for example, for instance*
Particularisation	*especially, in particular*
Concession	*granted that, it is true that*
Amplification	*also, furthermore, in addition, moreover, too*
Insistence	*in fact, indeed*
Restatement	*in other words, to put it another way, that is to say*
Recapitulation	*all in all, in conclusion, to summarise*
Time or place	*above, elsewhere, so far, subsequently*

Table 4 Using disjuncts

Type of disjunct	Examples	Illustration in use
Hearsay disjuncts:	*allegedly, reportedly*	'Reportedly, Virginia Woolf was particularly fond of this novel . . .'
Evidential disjuncts:	*clearly, obviously*	'Clearly it would be rash to assume that Wilde knew of this earlier version.'
Attitudinal disjuncts (less common but sometimes useful)	*unfortunately, sadly, luckily,* etc.	'Sadly, this was the last poem Wilfred Owen was to write . . .'

connectives relates to the list above. Formal markers of cohesion are not always necessary; but where you find sentences without them, it is a good idea to inspect them closely to check that the relationship with the preceding sentence is sufficiently clear.

Do not think, though, that simply because you put in cohesive devices the logical or rhetorical relationships of your essay are adequately constructed. It is possible to use cohesive markers that are incompatible with the sentences they are supposed to link. In such cases, the resulting effect is one of a cohesive text that nevertheless remains incoherent.

Disjuncts

Alongside the sorts of connective listed in Table 3, other kinds of link between sentences or sections of material can also be useful. Sometimes a **disjunct** can be used: a word or phrase that tells your reader what your attitude or degree of commitment is towards the material you present. Table 4 lists some types of disjunct with examples and illustrations.

Be careful with attitudinal disjuncts; they sometimes have an odd effect on the register of your essay, pulling it away from an expected level of formality. They are also usually used without the idea or sentiment they indicate being justified by any specific argument, which is another reason not to use them; for example, when you say 'unfortunately', you are claiming that something would have been better otherwise, without explicitly saying why (see Unit 9).

MEDIATING ESSAY MATERIAL FOR THE READER

As well as holding your text together, cohesive markers and disjuncts are tools for managing your essay, or standing back from it and presenting what you have written to your reader. By commenting directly on the organisation of your essay you can direct your reader to specific parts of it, perhaps for emphasis; and you can comment on your material. This process is usually referred to as **mediation**, or acting as a go-between, or guide.

Mediating devices include phrases like, 'as I have shown above', 'so far I have tried to argue that', 'it may be helpful here to distinguish between', 'in my introductory paragraph', etc. Mediation can also be achieved by means of brief summaries of what has gone before, or even by direct repetition of key points – though repetition must be clearly for the benefit of the reader, not just to fill up space.

As with markers of structure, it is unwise to over-use mediating devices, especially where they involve direct repetition. But in our experience, this kind of **metacommentary** (meaning 'commentary on what you are doing') tends to be under-used in essays at all levels from A-level through to PhD. Readers are left to struggle for too many connections and linkages on their own.

MAKING LOCAL EDITS

We conclude this unit with some practical suggestions about using word-processing tools to implement editing decisions. Software tools such as 'cut, copy and paste', editing in 'outline view', and 'track changes' make manipulating or altering your draft quick and easy; but it is also important to remember that such tools are simply powerful ways of performing operations that can still be done without them. If you are temporarily away from a machine, or if you don't have access to a computer at all, this does not mean that you can't edit. The tasks may take far longer and be less easy; but it is the strategic choices you make, rather than your tools for implementing those choices, which move the process of writing an essay forward.

Cut, copy and paste

It is unlikely that all the sentences you write will stay in the same place in your essay, from the time you first think of them through to the completed version. You should therefore expect to manipulate your draft substantially. By cutting and pasting you can, for example, shift general material into topic-sentence position from somewhere inside a paragraph, or insert quotations or case studies at relevant points.

Within sentences, you should also consider possibilities for moving words or phrases, so that the beginning of your sentence has a more evident link or overlap with the preceding sentence, and what comes at the end of your sentence is new for this sentence and also links forward to the point you make next.

Some of your edits, however, will require moving larger sections of material. Where you decide to move whole sections, remember that you can move text attached to headings in outline view in programs such as Microsoft® Word (see Unit 7); and by using this powerful editing tool, you can combine the test of structure discussed above – reading through headings to ensure they signal a coherent, overall argument – with actually moving sections of your draft to bring that coherent argument into being.

Use colour

As you add or modify text, it is possible to change its colour; and while you are very unlikely to want to print in colour, you can use colour on the screen as an easy visual cue. You might, for example, put section headings of different levels in different colours; or you might add comments in blue. Or you might colour red any parts of the text that you are not sure about and think you will need to come back to. Remember that when you use the search function in a word-processor, you can usually search by colour. So if you have put all the passages that will need later revision in red, you can do a final 'red' search to make sure you have revised all of them.

Track changes

When you make changes using word-processing software, most edits are non-destructive: you can reverse a change if you don't like it by using the 'undo' function. What 'undo' doesn't allow you to do, however, is to look simultaneously at your earlier draft and at the annotations you are making or deciding between. One way of doing that is to use a function like 'track changes' in Microsoft® Word.

Track changes records changes and, like using colour more generally, allows you to highlight them on-screen. Track changes shows edits by visibly striking through deleted text, presenting added material in colour, and labelling each change with the date it was made and which computer user made it (something that is especially useful if you are co-writing). By activating track changes you can review layers of successive revision, and quickly accept or reject each change as appropriate.

KEEP EARLIER DRAFTS OR DISCARD THEM?

As you edit your essay, you accumulate a large number of drafts, fragments, lists of examples and quotations, and other relevant material. The question then arises whether it is better to keep all this material – so that nothing gets lost – or whether you should discard it, to keep everything simple and in one place. The choice between these alternatives depends on your personal working preferences. And it needn't be a clear-cut choice, one or the other, since it is possible to keep a selection of drafts while discarding earlier experiments that no longer contain anything likely to be incorporated.

There are several factors to weigh up. It is sensible, for example, to keep all your drafts if you are working on a word-processor that can store them easily, sorted with details of date originated and date most recently edited. In any case, you certainly need to keep a back-up copy at different stages, preferably separate from the machine you generally work on. Apart from your own distress if you lose files, tutors tend to be unsympathetic to lost files and corrupted disks; they can do little to help and have no way of establishing how justified your account of the relevant circumstances is.

There are, however, some slightly less obvious reasons for *not* keeping all your drafts. Once drafts proliferate, there are too many overlapping documents to read and organise. There is also the risk of revising something in a draft that doesn't contain all the other changes you want to retain, since they were made to a different draft. You can then end up with multiple, parallel drafts that, to be useful at all, have to be painstakingly synthesised. Perhaps more importantly, too, keeping all your options open by keeping all your drafts postpones making decisions – sometimes until so much material has accumulated that it is difficult to maintain a coherent, overall view of what decisions you need to make.

Editing is a process of making changes; keeping earlier versions allows a set of those changes to accumulate. But it is also a matter of making decisions. Burning bridges once you have crossed them (keeping back-ups separate and only for use if you suffer a serious setback such as a computer crash) can help you focus on achieving a final, single version to hand in.

EXERCISE

We have suggested that passages of text may seem incoherent because cohesive markers have been used that are incompatible with the sentences they are supposed to link. Consider in this light the use of 'however' in the final sentence of the following:

> It is unlikely that Shakespeare or the majority of writers in construction of their work imagined the twentieth-century reader or considered the possibility that the reader would be of another race or colour than his own (the exception to this assumption can be found in later twentieth-century writers). However, Shakespeare wrote *Othello*.

'However' here seems to create a slightly odd effect. Describe as clearly as you can the contrast that appears to be intended. Then consider whether any other contrast emerges from the choice of 'however' as the connective here: formulate as precisely as you can the two ideas you feel are being contrasted.

EDITING THE BEGINNING AND ENDING

In the previous unit, we considered how to edit your work so that each point you make has clear links to your overall essay structure. We now consider two especially important – because they are especially prominent – sections of any piece of written work: the beginning and the ending. The beginning has to create interest and tell the reader what to expect; the ending forms a disproportionate part of the reader's final impression, not only because it is read last but because it is assumed to sum up and bring your essay to a significant conclusion. When it comes to the marking of your essay, your marker may start the process of deciding the final mark when they read the first paragraph, and may reach a final decision while reading the final paragraph; so these two paragraphs probably have proportionally the most impact on your mark. We also illustrate difficulties that arise with several common types of beginnings and endings, and suggest how you can avoid them.

PARTICULAR PROMINENCE: THE FIRST PARAGRAPH

The first paragraph of your essay tells your reader what the essay will be about: what its main focus is, and what question or questions you are going to answer. But your first paragraph is also an opportunity to start working actively on those questions. This is true even if you are writing on a prescribed question (perhaps in an exam); in such cases, you can re-formulate the question in your first paragraph to demonstrate that you have understood it and can build arguments from it.

Stating the main point

Here is an example of a set question:

> Explain fully the significance of the title of 'The Captain's Doll'.

And here is the beginning of an essay which answers it:

> The significance of the title of 'The Captain's Doll' is its use as a central symbol or motif which is the organising principle for the whole story. Though the doll motif can be applied to several different characters, its central meaning is a representation of that which Lawrence dislikes in relationships between men and women.

The essay begins by stating its main point: that the title focuses attention on a multi-functional symbol within the story. But to do this, the writer simply repeats the wording of the question, which throws away the opportunity to speak in his or her own voice at this crucial initial moment. Instead the writer could have used material from the question to begin the essay with a generalisation (Unit 9), like this:

> Titles often serve the purpose of focusing attention on a central symbol; and this is certainly true of 'The Captain's Doll'. Though the doll motif . . .

Just repeating the question tells your examiner nothing about what you know, but still takes up time and space. Reworking the question into a related generalisation, on the other hand, shows that you understand something of the complexities it contains and can place your reading of the work in question in the context of other works and general approaches to literature (Unit 8). Similarly, by reformulating the question in your first sentence you begin to show your understanding that key terms in the question are problematic or vague; and you can suggest what kind of evidence you will draw on to discuss the question.

Explaining the essay's structure or organisation

As well as introducing the content of your essay, your first paragraph should begin to explain its organisation. But don't overdo this by being too overt, as in this opening to an essay titled 'Lyrical and Epical Genres in Middle English Poetry':

> I shall begin discussing lyrical and epical genres in Middle English poetry with the explanation of both these terms. But before they will be explained it is necessary to consider the term genre. Quoting Burrow . . .

While this beginning is effective in showing organisation, it delays getting into the argument and indeed introduces a more general question than the one presented. It could be rewritten in the following way, which demonstrates organisation less clumsily and gets immediately to the point:

> Since the terms 'lyrical' and 'epic' present special difficulties when used of Middle English works, it is useful to introduce discussion of works of the period with a brief analysis of these two terms. And since the larger concept of 'genre', within which they play a part, is also problematic, my discussion of the two terms will be prefaced by a more general discussion of 'genre'. Interestingly, Burrow's suggestion is that . . .

The problem of introducing a general discussion of 'genre' before answering the question actually asked is still there; but in this revised version the passage now offers *reasons* for this organisation of the essay, and so connects the answer more directly with the question.

Linking themes together

Slightly different problems arise in our next example, though again they are related to the relationship between the various topics being introduced:

> The 'Sonnet on the Death of Mr Richard West' contains many half-rhymes and can be split into two groups, the octave and the sestet. The sonnet is an emotional elegy, and the tone is mournful. The author addresses the reader directly.

In this passage, three topics are introduced: the sonnet's form, its tone, and its mode of address. But no link is suggested between them, and it isn't yet clear what the main point of the essay will be. We could rewrite this opening as:

> In the 'Sonnet on the Death of Mr Richard West', formal qualities of the sonnet (such as its rhyme scheme, division between octave and sestet, and mode of address) are moulded to suit the mournful tone of an emotional elegy.

Now the individual observations are collected together under a common denominator (labelled 'formal qualities') and are linked to the claimed mood of the poem. Instead of just being presented with a list of topics, we are shown the relationship between those topics.

Introduction as a menu

A helpful first paragraph offers the reader a 'menu' of what will follow and at the same time begins the essay's argument. The menu should not be too large (some essays become front-heavy with preliminaries); and you should ensure that items on the menu are actually served up to the reader later. Subject areas outlined at the beginning are sometimes impossibly large, given the essay's pre-scribed length. It is therefore a good test of an opening sentence or paragraph to read it aloud, then list the topics you think it alerts a reader to expect, and make sure that those topics match your planned contents.

PARTICULAR PROMINENCE: THE LAST PARAGRAPH

Your reader pays particular attention to your last paragraph and last sentence because these bring the essay to a suitable conclusion. Sometimes a reader will read the last paragraph first in order to see what the essay says. 'A suitable conclusion', however, does not mean a repetition of your opening sentence. If you begin:

> In this essay, I will argue that Henry James's representations and frequent treatment of women through metaphors as art objects are deeply problematic.

then you should *not* end your essay by simply recapitulating:

> In the foregoing pages, I have shown how Henry James's representations and frequent treatment of women through metaphors as art objects are deeply problematic.

Such repetition is simply a reminder, not a conclusion. In a long dissertation it might be justified as a way of helping your reader remember how it began, and would in such circumstances be followed by a more genuine concluding point; in a short essay it is merely redundant and gives the impression that you have run out of new material but don't know how to finish.

What, then, should a 'suitable conclusion' look like? This depends on the aims of the essay, but it might include a judgement about which of the competing arguments you have discussed is correct or most persuasive. Alternatively, you might give an indication of what consequences follow from what you have shown in your essay. If you wish to end with consequences or implications, then consider whether there is anything you can say in answer to the following questions:

- Have you discovered any methods that can now be used to investigate another text or author?
- Does your argument suggest we should look again at some other area, which we might now view differently?
- Can you generalise what you have said to other works by the same author, by other authors, or to other works of the same period?
- Can you make any significant general observations, using your whole essay as an illustration or case study?

Each of these questions is made all the more worth exploring because final paragraphs and sentences often fall into one of a number of largely unsatisfactory idioms. Each suggests that bringing the essay to a close is less an opportunity than a means of escape. To show the difficulties of such idioms and how to avoid them, we conclude by illustrating and discussing four common, problematic endings.

The 'farewell speech'

Avoid the sort of ending used in this essay on 'Genres of the Old English Poetry':

> And in this way we have come to the end of our characterisation of the main genres of the oldest vernacular poetry in Western Europe; poetry which achieved so great variety over the 8th, 9th and 10th centuries.

The phrase 'come to the end of our' suggests a pleasant, shared experience or excursion; and the expression 'oldest vernacular poetry in Western Europe' calls to mind less the language of analysis or scholarship than that of advertising or publicity (where things are valued because they are the best, the oldest, etc.). These features of the style, coupled with the exclamatory force of 'so' ('so great variety') give an overall effect that the conclusion is a promotional, or uncritically praising, piece of writing rather than an academic study.

Indecisiveness disguised as fairness

Your essay is an argument; you should present that argument's different sides and positions. Your conclusion can then if you wish come to a decision on one side of the debate, and need not remain balanced. So avoid saying something like 'both sides have their virtues and it is difficult to decide between them'. It is perfectly acceptable to draw conclusions of your own, based on arguments and evidence you have presented. If you feel there is no clear-cut answer, then you should conclude by showing how you have weighed up different kinds of evidence. Either way, the challenge is to show that you have answered the question after giving fair consideration to all relevant positions.

Higher authority

When you write an essay you have both the opportunity *and* the responsibility to state your own views in your own words. It is often tempting to think that some critic could present your viewpoint better than you can yourself, and so to end your essay with a quotation from someone else. In Unit 13 we discuss using other people's words, and make the point there that one problem with other people's words is that they usually make more sense in their original context than they will in your essay. This is a general problem with quotation; but because your conclusion is so import-ant, it is usually better not to risk the slightly different emphases and directions that someone else's words are likely to carry when they are given this new context and prominence. The concerns of your essay will be different from those of the article or book you are quoting from, and this makes it unlikely that someone else's words will be exactly right as the conclusion to *your* argument.

Disconnected personal opinion

Concluding with your own words also requires caution, however, particularly in the handling of personal response. Despite the instruction often given by teachers to emphasise personal involvement towards the end of an essay, you should avoid the sort of over-personalised ending to be found here:

> After reading the first paragraph, I didn't expect such an exciting story, but gradually I got more and more involved in the narrative and finally overwhelmed by this splendid spectacle, which I could vividly visualise.

This sudden introduction of personal involvement into an essay that was otherwise a dispassionate description is disruptive, and sounds as if the writer really wanted to write much more personally throughout (so indicating a kind of dissatisfaction with the essay as it stands).

BEGINNINGS, ENDINGS AND ESSAY STRUCTURE

In this unit, we have picked out two particularly significant sections of your essay and explored how to address difficulties that commonly arise with them. But we should stress that difficulties with beginnings and endings are in many cases symptoms of more general problems. So if you find that your efforts to write or edit a first paragraph are unsuccessful, or that you can't think how to bring your essay to a conclusion, it may be necessary to go back to your overall essay plan. That plan should remind you of where the essay is supposed to lead and why, and so help you formulate the paragraph in question.

Having a clear structure for your essay from the outset changes the process of writing your first and last paragraph. You can write the essay in almost any order you like, and assemble it as a whole afterwards. In most cases it won't make sense to write the last paragraph first, since the process of writing will generate ideas you will want to incorporate into your conclusion. But writing your first paragraph last, when you have finished the rest, certainly *is* one advantage of writing to a clear structure. At that point, you can definitely promise what the essay covers – because you have written it already. You can introduce your essay better once you know it.

EXERCISE

Consider this final sentence from an essay on the element of satire in the work of two dramatists:

Both playwrights succeed in mixing description with analysis which is conveyed in entertaining prose.

Confine yourself to thinking about the expressions used in this sentence, and identify potential difficulties with each of the following words or phrases:

'description', 'analysis', 'entertaining prose'

Use the commentaries we have given on examples above to help you rewrite this final sentence so that it avoids the difficulties you identify. (You can do this without knowing which plays or dramatists were being referred to in the original essay.)

INCORPORATING OTHER PEOPLE'S
WORDS INTO WHAT YOU WRITE

In writing a literary essay, you will almost certainly want at some point to incorporate someone else's words. Because your essays are often about texts, you will need to incorporate extracts from texts into your essay so that you can discuss them. And since your ideas about those texts always build on the ideas and discoveries of other people, you will sometimes want to report their words exactly.

QUOTATION AND PARAPHRASE

Quotation involves copying the words exactly as they were in the original text. **Paraphrase** involves selective rewriting while retaining key words and other parts of the original.

- Original by Patricia Craig:

> One of the most striking things about detective fiction is the ease with which it accommodates all kinds of topical ideologies.

- Quotation:

> 'One of the most striking things about detective fiction',
> Patricia Craig argues in her critical introduction to English
> detective stories, 'is the ease with which it accommodates
> all kinds of topical ideologies.'

- Paraphrase (or summary):

> It is among the most striking features of detective
> fiction, Patricia Craig points out, that all kinds of topical
> ideologies are easily accommodated within it.

- Mixture of paraphrase and quotation:

> One of the most striking features of detective fiction,
> as Patricia Craig points out, is the way in which it
> 'accommodates all kinds of topical ideologies.'

The most obvious difference between quotation and paraphrase in these examples is the punctuation that separates a quotation from the surrounding material. A paraphrase usually changes the language of the original, because all that matters is that the idea is conveyed, not the precise words in which it was originally formulated. When you need to use someone else's ideas you normally paraphrase rather than quote, because this is a way of rewriting the relevant material in a way that assimilates it into your essay and your own voice. In contrast, a quotation leaves the incorporated material sticking out because it is in a different style. As a general principle, try to be the author of as much of your essay as possible, rather than handing your text over to someone else (by quoting them). You should use a quotation mainly if the exact wording of the original is itself important.

Both quotation and paraphrase require that you identify the source (who wrote the original, and where it comes from). If you do not identify the source of a paraphrase you can still be accused of stealing someone else's ideas and words without acknowledging them (see section on plagiarism below). You should also tell the reader something about the context from which the quotation or paraphrase was taken, to indicate the background against which it is being used:

> In the course of a description of Henchard late in the novel, Hardy says, '[QUOTE]'

Quotations should not be left to speak on their own. A reasonable strategy is to assume that your reader will skip the quotations and expect you as the writer to extract for the reader everything that is relevant from the quotation. For this reason, you should add a commentary or gloss, clarifying the relevance of the quotation to your argument. Since quoted material can be read in many different ways, you need to make explicit how you intend it to be read, and the particular contribution the quotation makes. A lengthy quotation which is not then followed by detailed analysis and discussion is likely to seem inappropriately used as a way of replacing rather than supporting your argument; so you should guide your reader through the significance of what you have selected for their attention. Everything we have said here applies equally to pictures or other materials that you may incorporate into your essay.

Formatting quotations

Literary essays typically follow a simple set of conventions governing the presentation of quotations.

- Short quotations in prose (up to about 40 to 50 words) are incorporated in the body of the text, enclosed within single quotation marks. (Some systems recommend double quotation marks; either will be acceptable unless otherwise specified, so long as you are consistent.)
- Longer prose quotations are indented as a whole by about half an inch from the left margin of the rest of the text, and should *not* have quotation marks.

- Quotations in verse, if more than one line, are indented without quotation marks like longer prose quotations, and should be laid out as carefully as possible like the original.

Note that all quoted material should copy the spelling and punctuation of the source edition. If you omit words from a quotation, you should indicate the omission by the use of three points (= full-stops), allowing a blank space on either side. Any editorial insertions you make within a quotation should be enclosed within square brackets [ ].

> This tendency for the image of war to be *distorted* [my italics] has the effect of . . . encouraging unjustifiable patriotism.

INDICATING WHERE SOMEONE ELSE'S WORDS COME FROM

There are two basic alternative systems for indicating the source of a quotation, usually called the **notes (and bibliography)** system and the **author-date** system. Use one or the other, but do not mix them together. The information given in both systems is called 'bibliographic information' (or sometimes more generally **documentation**). We give examples in this section of references to three kinds of text: a book, a chapter in an edited book, and an article in a journal. There are other possibilities, which follow the same basic principles (see also the exercise at the end of this unit).

'Notes' or 'notes and bibliography' system

This is the 'traditional' system for bibliographic information for literature essays. In this system, a note gives the bibliographic information. Usually this is a footnote. There are two variants, illustrated below: either all the information is given in the footnote, or the footnote gives a brief version of the information (author's surname/family name, brief title, page reference) and a bibliography at the end of the essay gives the full version of the information.

1. Version in which the footnote gives all the information for a quotation. The number at the end is the page number of the book. There is no supplementary bibliography required in conjunction with the footnote.

1. Kathleen M. Briggs, *A Dictionary of British Folk Tales in the English Language* (London: Routledge, 1970), 136.
2. Kristin Hanson and Paul Kiparsky. 'A Parametric Theory of Poetic Meter,' *Language* 72 (1996), 295.
3. Bruce Hayes, 'The Prosodic Hierarchy in Meter.' In Paul Kiparsky and Gilbert Youmans, eds, *Phonetics and Phonology 1: Rhythm and meter* (San Diego: Academic Press, 1989), 255.

2. Brief version in which the footnote gives partial information:

1. Briggs *Dictionary of British Folk Tales*, 136.
2. Hanson and Kiparsky 'Parametric Theory', 295
3. Hayes 'Prosodic Hierarchy', 255.

This brief version is then supplemented by an entry in a bibliography at the end of the essay, which looks like this (note that the page reference for the quotation is not given in the bibliography, since it was given in the footnote; page numbers in the bibliography refer to the pages on which the whole article or chapter is to be found).

Briggs, Kathleen M. *A Dictionary of British Folk Tales in the English Language*. London: Routledge, 1970.
Hanson, Kristin and Paul Kiparsky. 'A Parametric Theory of Poetic Meter,' *Language* 72 (1996): 287–335.
Hayes, Bruce 'The Prosodic Hierarchy in Meter.' In Paul Kiparsky and Gilbert Youmans, eds, *Phonetics and Phonology 1: Rhythm and meter* (San Diego: Academic Press,1989): 201–260.

The word *ibid.* is sometimes used in a note which quotes the same book as an immediately preceding note (sometimes in a sequence of notes all of which quote from the same book). For example you might have as a fourth footnote, a reference to page 258 of the same chapter by Hayes.

> 4. Ibid., 258.

Author-date system

This system (sometimes also called the **Harvard** system, or the **name plus date** style) is used in social science (and linguistics) publications and essays, as well as increasingly in literature essays. This system incorporates the reference into the text (usually in brackets) and requires a bibliography at the end to give full information. The in-text reference includes just the surname/family name of the author and the date of the work you are referring to, plus where appropriate the page reference – crucially you do *not* include the title of the work. The lack of the title is the most significant difference between this and the note system, where at a minimum a short title for the text being referred to is given.

To refer to the same sources cited above, you would put the following after the quotation:

> (Briggs 1970, 136)
> (Hanson and Kiparsky 1996, 295)
> (Hayes 1989, 255)

You would then add a bibliographic reference at the end of the essay, in the list of references, which would give the remaining information. (We return to final bibliographies in Unit 15.)

This system identifies a work by its author and date (hence the name of the system); but there may be cases where you wish to refer to two works by the same author published in the same year. If this is the case, the two works are differentiated by adding letters, as in (Lane 2001a) and (Lane 2001b); the letters are indicated both in the in-text reference and in the bibliography. If there are two authors with the same name, then you include an initial to indicate the first name as well as the surname. You don't need to indicate explicitly in the in-text reference whether the surname is that of an author or an editor; and you can use 'et al' to stand for several names if you wish. If the text is anonymous, you can use a short title of the text in place of the surname instead of saying 'anon'.

Principles underlying reference systems

You may have been given explicit instruction which reference system to use; if so, follow the system prescribed. If not, choose whichever one you prefer, but be consistent in what you do. You use references in order to give credit to people whose words or ideas you use, and to enable your reader to find the original sources if necessary. You may find that you need to refer to kinds of work other than books or articles; for example, to a website, film or performance. There are published guides to referring to these, but for the kinds of essays you are writing (i.e. coursework essays, rather than for academic articles in journals), we suggest that you invent your own formula for referring to them in a way that achieves these general objectives (and try the exercise at the end of this unit).

PLAGIARISM

Plagiarism is when you do not properly acknowledge the source of the ideas or phrases in your essay as you should (i.e. by giving a reference formulated along the lines indicated above). Instead, other people's ideas and words are passed off as your own.

Apart from the ethical problem plagiarism involves – it is a kind of theft – it can also disrupt your writing. Usually, as well as copying, plagiarism involves adapting a text you have found, for example by taking isolated sentences, omitting words and phrases, and replacing some words with other words that seem to you to mean the same. One typical consequence of local changes made in this way, however, is that the piece of text you end up producing is disjointed, sometimes becoming a passage that no longer makes sense because of the alterations you have introduced. Alongside this loss of sense, too, the process of plagiarising has a further side-effect: that the alterations imposed on the original usually jut out with painful obviousness from other parts of the essay that you really wrote yourself.

How can plagiarism happen by accident?

Many or perhaps even most cases of plagiarism are probably accidents. But because it is difficult for markers to judge whether plagiarism is accidental or deliberate, they tend to penalise all plagiarism in the same way, whether it was intended or not. For this reason it is important to understand how accidental plagiarism can occur and to guard against it.

- You find an essay on the internet that you think you can use, and copy or download part of it. Then you paste the material you have downloaded into the essay you submit. The problem arises when you forget to indicate a source for the pasted-in material. (Material plagiarised from the internet can in principle be easy for your marker to find, incidentally, by using a search engine to look for any unusual phrase in your essay.)
- You take notes from a book, but when you do so, you forget to indicate in your notes that the material comes from somewhere else and is not something you thought of yourself. Later, when you look at your notes you think the words are your own and you just incorporate them into your essay.
- You work with someone else on a prescribed essay topic you are both doing, and take shared notes, with the result that each of you is drawing on the same words and phrases. Then you both submit essays that look as though one is copied from the other. In this case, you should protect yourself by indicating in the essay when ideas and words come from a shared discussion or from a process of collaborative research.

There are other varieties of 'accidental plagiarism' besides these, but they all arise in broadly the same way. There is some kind of separation between taking notes and writing the essay, and when you took the notes you failed to indicate clearly which words or ideas came from someone else; then by the time you write the essay you have forgotten.

To guard against accidental plagiarism that can arise when taking notes or downloading material:

- Always mark direct quotations by putting the material in quotation marks and keep a note of the source. Anything more than a word that you copy should be noted in this way.
- Clearly indicate in your note when an idea comes from or is even inspired by someone else. This will actually improve the overall quality of your work, and may get you a better mark because it indicates that you are developing your ideas in relation to other people's ideas, as academic work is supposed to.
- Distinguish clearly between paraphrase and quotation when you write your essay. If you paraphrase, try to rewrite completely, rather than embedding fragments of the original text in your new sentences.

EXERCISE

In answering the following questions, bear in mind the fundamental principle of documentation: you need to be able to refer as precisely as possible to a specific text (so that in principle someone else can find the original part of the text you are using).

1. How would you refer to a piece of text (e.g. a quotation from a text) that is in a medium other than writing on the page? Invent a system, based on the note-and-bibliography system, for citing as a source (i) an episode of a television programme, (ii) a film, (iii) a DVD or videocassette recording of a film.

2. Now consider transient or time-bound sources, such as performances and internet pages (which can be changed or deleted at any time). Invent a system (i) for referring to a performance of a play, and (ii) for referring to an internet page.

MISTAKES IN SPELLING, GRAMMAR
AND PUNCTUATION

No-one owns English, and no-one has a natural right to tell other English speakers how to use it. People do publish prescriptive grammar books, as well as dictionaries which tell you how to spell words and style manuals that tell you how to punctuate; when they do this, however, they are either making their own choice between different possible (in many cases, arbitrary) rules or else they are conforming to rules that have been selected at some point by other people from a range of possibilities and passed down through history. Of course, just because a rule could have been different doesn't mean you should ignore it. If you ignore the rule that tells you to drive down the left-hand side of the road in Britain you may crash your car. Similarly, you can 'crash' your essay by breaking the most influential – though finally arbitrary, simply conventional – rules of writing.

WHAT MAKES SOMETHING A MISTAKE AND WHY DOES IT MATTER?

Here are four sentences which contain fairly typical mistakes.

> (a) In a manner when this writer demonstrates that the female characters will overcome their detractors.
> (b) She has underwent a great deal of unhappiness.
> (c) Laterally Anne became critically ill.
> (d) This poem demonstrates it's intentions immediately.

Sentence (a) has as its mistake the fact that it is a subordinate clause and not a full sentence; (a) should be inside another sentence, not on its own. There are two reasons the mistake matters, and so should be avoided. First, it makes the sentence difficult to understand because there is something missing (perhaps something which another sentence would provide). Second, your marker will take it as evidence that you are a poor writer and that you do not proofread (as these kinds of mistake can usually be easily discovered).

Sentence (b) has as its mistake the combination of words *has underwent*, instead of *has undergone*. The mistake here relates to standard and non-standard forms of English. In standard English *underwent* is used only as a past form (**preterite**) as in *he underwent*. In non-standard English (e.g. in the Scottish dialect used here), *underwent* is also used as a participle form; here a non-standard form is being used in an academic essay. Linguists, who analyse the structure of languages, do not prefer standard to non-standard forms, and argue that all dialects of a language are equally grammatical and regular. There is nevertheless social pressure to use standard forms, particularly in academic essays. So this is a 'social mistake' and not a linguistic one.

Sentence (c) has as its mistake the word *laterally* instead of *latterly*. Both are real words of English but this is clearly a spelling mistake: *latterly* has been spelled as *laterally*. This kind of mistake falls into the class of 'mistakes involving double letters', and is probably encouraged by two things: (i) the fact that the word *later* is contained in *laterally*, and (ii) there might be some 'cross-infection' from the word *critically* later in the same sentence. While it is easy enough for your reader to understand what you meant, the problem with this mistake is that your reader is likely to find it funny; spelling mistakes, particularly of non-technical terms like this, can also be taken as indicating ignorance.

Sentence (d) has as its mistake the use of *it's* as a possessive word instead of *its*. In some ways this is one of the most interesting mistakes it is possible to make. Partly this is because it is very common: it turns up in print and on signs and notices as well as in student essays. It is also easy to see why people make the mistake – it seems to make sense to add *'s* onto the word *it*, though in fact this isn't the structure of the word (as we explain below). It is such a common mistake that we might ask whether it should even be considered a mistake. Perhaps speakers of English should all agree to write the word *it's* instead; but until they do, the existing convention remains in place.

All of these mistakes come down to the same thing. Someone else, at some time, made up a convention for how to write, and you need to know what it is. None of these conventions had to be as they are; everything might have been different (even writing a sentence without a finite verb could have been a legitimate writing practice). On the whole your marker will know the conventions, however, and may penalise you for not knowing them. There is also a further complication: sometimes it is not a matter of correct and incorrect (i.e. a mistake), but something that might be 'more' or 'less' correct. Usually in such cases there are widespread legitimate variations, perhaps where one spelling is ousting another as part of a process of historical change.

Why are English words difficult to spell?

English words are difficult to spell. It is possible to learn exceptionless rules for spelling, though the only one people usually remember is the rule 'i before e except after c', which gives you *sieve* but *conceive*. Such rules-without-exceptions are rare (hence our one example); generally learning how to spell is a word-by-word matter.

Why has English ended up in this state, where it is so difficult to predict from its sound how a word is spelled? The answer comes from the complex history both of the English vocabulary and the English sound-system. English words have come from many different sources, and sometimes carry 'sound-spelling' conventions with them from those different sources. Furthermore, the conventional spellings of many English words were established several hundred years ago, after which there have been significant changes in how English sounds. And finally, there are not enough vowel letters in English (five: a, e, i, o, u) to capture all the different vowel sounds in English (which varies between dialects, but usually has about ten distinct vowels, and many vowel-combinations called diphthongs).

This means that in English the relation between vowel letters and vowel sounds is especially complex; and even though the relationship is generally systematic, it is usually simpler to learn sound-spelling correspondences on a word-by-word basis.

This all means that learning how to spell is a matter of memory, not intelligence. In some ways, therefore, it is a pity that spelling mistakes are stigmatised in the way they are, since they are an understandable response to the complexity of sound-spelling correspondences in English; and in any case they rarely impede understanding. Still, they do carry the stigma of being a poor writer and imply that you are also an inexperienced reader (because you did not spot your own mistake, and appear not to have learned the correct spelling from your reading experience).

Some ways to monitor your spelling

Learning how to spell is partly a matter of becoming sensitive to when something might be wrong, and being willing to look it up. You can also learn strategies for monitoring your spelling as a way of helping you to become sensitive to possible errors. But it is always necessary to check by looking up, even with a strategy; strategies will rarely just give you the right answer. Spellings can be conveniently looked up in dictionaries which just list words (without definitions), such as a dictionary of pronunciation.

Related words have related spellings (sometimes)

A commonly mis-spelled word is *repetition*, often spelled as *repitition (the asterisk here indicates a mis-spelling). One way to remember that the second vowel in *repetition* is *e* is to consider the related word *repeat*, which has an *e* (as part of *ea*) but does not have *i*. The word *grammar* is often mis-spelled as *grammer*; one way to remember that there is an *a* is that the vowel in this position is unmistakably written as an *a* in *grammatical*. The word *existence* is commonly mis-spelled as *existance*; but the related word *existential* shows that the relevant vowel is *e*. In each case, you use a word that is easy to spell as a guide to a word that is less easy to spell. You still need to check in a dictionary if you aren't sure, but if you have a complex word you might look at the words it contains. Early in this unit we looked at the word *laterally* as a mis-spelling of *latterly*. It is possible that the writer saw the word *later* in this word and thought that it was the base of *laterally*; but they could also have spotted that the word contains the quite unintended *lateral*. In fact *latterly* is based on *latter* (not *later*).

Double or single letter?

The mistake involving *laterally* instead of *latterly* also involves double letters. These are a standard source of error, and something you should check if you are not sure. For example, the word *parallel* is often mis-spelled (e.g. as **paralell*). Why are the letters doubled where they are? In this case, the answer is probably historical, and relates to the spelling of the Greek (and later Latin and French) words from which *parallel* derives, all of which have double l followed by single l. The best way to remember this is either just to learn it or possibly to remember it by associating it with some other word, such as the similarly spelled and related word *allele* (a genetic term, memorable because not often encountered in general usage).

American vs British spelling variations

American spelling and British spelling differ in various ways, usually because of an innovation in one but not the other country. The most significant difference is that Americans tend to use the (historically older) -ize form in a word such as *modernize*, while British spellers either use the more recent -ise as in *modernise* or alternatively follow the American pattern. Another divergence involves words such as American *meter* and British *metre*. Other differences involve 'simplifications' which were introduced by the lexicographer Noah Webster, such as American *labor* (British *labour*) and American *modeler* (British *modeller*).

PROBLEMS WITH GRAMMAR

We now turn to some common mistakes in grammar (or **syntax**, the combination of words into phrases and into a sentence).

The subject of a sentence and its relation with the verb

An English sentence generally starts with a phrase which is called the **subject** of the sentence and has a special relation with the verb.

Agreement

This special relation is seen in the use of a special form of the verb when the subject is 'third person singular'. The verb is said to **agree** with the subject and ends in the suffix -s (if it is a regular verb). In principle this should not present a problem, as speakers of English perform this 'agreement' automatically and unconsciously. But there are two complications. First, in some spoken dialects of English there is no agreement, which creates a split between the non-standard dialect and the need to write standard English. Second, and more significantly, written sentences sometimes have a level of complexity that can lead to some disconnection in writing between subject and verb, such that agreement fails.

Here are some examples where a mistake results from the subject failing to agree with the verb. The head noun in the subject is emboldened, the verb is underlined.

> **Advocates** of Northrop-Frye-style genre analysis <u>believes</u> . . .

The subject here is plural (it is headed by *advocates*) but there is a singular noun *analysis* close to the verb, which is incorrectly taken to be the subject.

The following sentence shows a slightly different (but also common) agreement error.

> This unit deals with **the different linguistic choices** that <u>shapes</u> women's magazine advertisements.

Shapes should agree with *choices* (i.e. it should be **choices** that *shape*), but the intervening *that* seems to have interfered, as though *that* is being taken as the (singular) subject.

A third common agreement error involves sentences that begin with *There is* or *There are*, with the real subject shifted to later in the sentence. It is this shifted subject which decides whether the verb is singular *is* or plural *are*:

> In some cases there *was* plenty of **references** to the protagonist's body parts.

Here the verb should have been <u>*were*</u> because of *references* being plural.

A verb needs the right subject

Another common error involving the match between subject and verb involves verbs that 'lose' their subject, such as the verb *having* in the following sentence.

> Having discussed this poem's beginning, the next stanza shows a marked change of mood.

The writer means that she has discussed the poem's meaning, but the sentence literally says that the next stanza discusses the poem's beginning (an unintended meaning). This is because *the next stanza* is interpreted as the subject of the verb. Compare the next sentence in which there is no mistake.

> *Encouraged* by the success of her early publications, Charlotte Bronte gave over increased amounts of time to writing.

Here, by contrast, it is Charlotte Bronte who is the implied subject of *encouraged*; and she is also the grammatical subject of the sentence.

Tense, and the finite verb

A **finite verb** is a verb which expresses the tense of the sentence – that is, whether it refers to an event in the past, present or future. (There are some technicalities here which we must skip over.) A typical error in writing is to have a full sentence (i.e. a sentence beginning with a capital letter and ending in a full stop) which lacks a finite verb.

Choosing present or past tense

If your verbs show tense, you have to choose which one. But should you use present tense or past tense in your writing? In general, you use the present tense to describe a text, or what an author did when they wrote the text. The basic idea here is that you are describing the text in terms of its present state.

> In *Los Gusanos* (1991) John Sayles describes Miami as it was in the early 1980s. He constructs a complex set of interrelationships between the different ethnic groups.

It would sound odd to put this description into the past tense, with 'described' and 'constructed', unless you were deliberately emphasising the fact that this book was produced at a particular point in the past, for example in order to compare it explicitly with a book written more recently. The present tense is generally also used when telling a story, as in a summary of the narrative of a novel. The present tense is used in this case because it carries a sense of immediacy and impact. Past tense, on the other hand, is generally used for describing situations or narrating events *outside* the work(s) you are discussing, such as those of national or cultural history or the development of literary traditions. Once you have decided which tense to use for a particular section of your essay, check that you are consistent – do not for example start a narrative summary in one tense and later change into another.

PUNCTUATION AND THE BOUNDARIES OF THE SENTENCE: FULL STOP, COMMA AND SEMI-COLON

Full stop and semi-colon

A full written sentence (containing a finite verb) begins with a capital letter and ends with a full stop ('full stop' is called 'period' in

American English). A full written sentence can contain two or more sub-sentences (clauses). Where the two sub-sentences could in principle be written as two separate sentences, you can use a semi-colon.

> The next verse is significantly longer than the first; this can be understood as a symbolic representation of the importance of its contents.

The rule for semi-colons is that they can always be replaced by full stops (capitalising the next letter):

> The next verse is significantly longer than the first. This can be understood as a symbolic representation of the importance of its contents.

Where the two sub-sentences *cannot* be separated in this way, you should use a comma.

> Although she was a mentally ill person who lived in her own mind and was allocated a limited number of mental processes, she was determined to act, to do something about this predator.

Here we cannot replace the comma by a full stop; the first sentence is not complete on its own:

> *Although she was a mentally ill person who lived in her own mind and was allocated a limited number of mental processes. She was determined to act, to do something about this predator.

Comma

The comma is used to separate off various supplementary elements in a sentence.

- Put a comma between two complete sentences where the second sentence begins with 'and', 'but', or 'or' (though this usage varies depending on the 'dialect' of written English you use):

> This is Dickens's final comment, and in future he avoided the topic of school education.

- Put a comma to separate a comment such as the following:

> *Whenever she leaves the house,* the heroine seems to become bolder.

> Lawrence concentrated on writing rather than painting, *which was fortunate.*

- Commas can be used to separate off a parenthetical, as in the following:

> Melville's great novel, *Moby Dick,* is in many ways a troublesome one.

> The pagan, *who with his tattoos and shrunken heads appears to be a terrible savage in the beginning,* turns out to be the most noble character in the novel.

Many writers incorrectly put a comma only before the parenthetical element (the extra, inserted phrase or clause) and forget to put one after it as well. Generally, when you wish to punctuate a piece of optional, additional information or an aside that you are embedding in the middle of a sentence – for example with commas, dashes or brackets – then whatever punctuation you use should be placed both before and after the added element to signal its boundaries, not just at one end or the other.

In many cases, despite the existence of general conventions it remains a writer's personal decision whether to use a comma or not. Some people like using commas and others prefer not to. Commas help your reader to understand the structure of a sentence, but like any other kind of detailed structuring they risk interfering with reading instead of helping it. Punctuation has sometimes been used to imitate the pauses a speaker might make if reading a sentence aloud, and commas often keep something of this function still. As an example of how punctuation rules work, consider the rule that forbids you inserting a comma to separate the subject and the verb. Despite this rule, writers commonly do this, as can be seen from the following examples:

The quasi-totality of students in my department, *opted* for English . . .

However, a close analysis of his individual texts, *has been under-researched* . . .

Existing biographical, historical, and philosophical works on Oscar Wilde, *have enhanced* our knowledge and understanding of his literary personality . . .

These are interesting cases of punctuation. It is possible that the writers may have decided, in each case, that the rule had to be broken in order to help the reader follow the sentence. Evidently in each sentence the purpose of the comma is to tell you that an unusually long subject has finished and that the verb is about to follow.

Another place where writers put commas 'illegally' is between a verb which describes saying and the sentence which presents what is said:

. . . what John Clarke *calls*, 'the subcultural bricoleurs . . .

This example is an interesting one because different people have different views about whether or not it is in fact 'illegal'. The writer probably used a comma here in imitation of a similar kind of example, 'John Clarke said, "these are subcultural bricoleurs . . ."'.

We ourselves would not have used a comma in the example above because we think in that example there is a greater degree of interdependence between the parts of the sentence than in the otherwise similar case it seems to imitate. In the next rather similar example, however, we think it is much clearer that the comma is a mistake and far less likely that it is simply a style variant:

> This has the implication *that*, novel writing in Wales . . .

The writer probably added a comma to indicate that a new sentence is starting. But this comma confusingly hides the close grammatical relation between 'implication that' and the sentence which follows.

Apostrophe and s

It's and Its
The word *it's* with an apostrophe is used only as an informal way of writing *it is*. If you have the word *it's* in your sentence, try replacing it with *it is*. If the result is nonsense, you have written the word wrongly; you should have written *its* instead.

> 'The century reached it's end.'
> > *'The century reached it is end.'
> So here you should have written 'The century reached its end.'

The word *its* is the possessive form of the word *it*, and is equivalent to the words *his* and *her* (and *their, my, your,* etc.). Note in particular that *his* is not written as *hi's* (or *he's*), and for the same reason this form of *its* does not have an apostrophe either. This is such a common mistake that it would be possible to dispute whether it is a mistake at all, as we discussed earlier. The mistake is also quite logical: a possessive word like *its* seems to have the same relation to *it* as the possessive word *John's* has to *John*.

Other problems with apostrophe s

Apostrophe s causes several other less common problems. First, people are sometimes unsure how to deal with a word that ordinarily ends in s, such as the name Keats. Here the possessive form is definitely not *Keat's*, but it is generally considered acceptable either to write *Keats'* or *Keats's*. Second, apostrophe s is sometimes used – incorrectly – to indicate a plural. So someone might write *The poem's are all sonnets*, which should be *The poems are all sonnets*. Third, dates should be written as *the 1920s* not *the 1920's*. Finally, plural words which end in the plural suffix -s should have the apostrophe at the end of the word: *the horses' mouths* not *the horse's mouths*.

EXERCISE

The following passage, which is the closing section of an essay on the central issues raised by Shakespeare's play *Hamlet*, contains a number of spelling, punctuation and grammatical errors. Using suitable reference sources if necessary, correct the mistakes in the way you might do going through a piece of your own writing before submitting it. At the same time, tidy up the presentation in other ways suggested in this and previous units.

> Hamlet is up against not just a man, but a king, he will have to strike when the king is unarmed, And he would also have to be able to explain his actions, and yet even his mother does not believe him, but only see him as mad
>
> 'Hamlet thou has't cleft my heart in twain.'
>
> To conclude, the play does give us the answers to the questions we demand from Hamlet, we understand the delay's he makes in killing Claudius due to the nature of his thoughts, he is concerned with the future of his soul and this seems to me the central issue in Shakespeare's *Hamlet*.

HANDING IN

All things come to an end. In this unit we look at how you make the process of finishing your essay or dissertation and handing it in as straightforward as possible.

MEETING YOUR DEADLINE

With essays, things often seem to go wrong at the very end, so we begin this unit by suggesting some ways of protecting yourself.

If you are writing on a computer, keep multiple back-up copies of what you are doing, perhaps a copy at the end of each day. If you have no physical mechanism for doing this (e.g. a removable flash drive, floppy disk, etc.) then e-mail a copy to yourself as an attachment, to be picked up next day, or use the free storage space that most internet providers will give you. Keeping back-ups will help you if your computer breaks down (you drop it, drop something onto it, it gets a virus, or it just takes a strange turn).

If your printer breaks down and you need to use a different printer with another computer, consider saving your file for printing elsewhere as just a text file or as a .pdf file (i.e. generic, rather than in some particular word-processing programme). It may not look as nice but it should be essentially the same.

If you have to send in your work by post, either get a receipt of mailing, or send the work as an e-mail attachment to your marker. Your marker probably won't want to be sent e-mailed files in general (you are increasing their workload, and making them use their time and ink for your essay), but simply as a guarantee that you have finished (and in advance of a printed version) it may be acceptable.

You can prepare yourself for unexpected problems in the closing stages by finding out where your school or university has open-access computers and printers, and what media (floppy disks, USB removable drives, etc.) these machines will accept. Remember that uploading to an internet site from your own computer and then downloading to another machine is also a possibility; learn how to do this before you need to. Find out what the rules are for late sub-mission, including whether and how you can get an extension and when this must be applied for.

Finally, if you do lose work, treat it as an opportunity, not a tragedy. Rewriting is generally a good thing, and your memories of what you lost will help filter the good parts in what you wrote – which you will remember – from the rest which originally padded it out; the result is quite often that your rewritten version turns out to be a simpler and sharper piece.

JUDGING WHEN YOUR ESSAY IS FINISHED

Literary studies is an open-ended activity. One of your main goals is to discover problems and work through them, and many literary texts will present problems that simply multiply and become more complex as you work more intensively with them. This is one of the reasons why it can be difficult to bring your writing to an end. Writing an essay involves trying to pull something coherent out of this complexity. So one way of considering 'completion' is to ask: 'have I answered the question I raised at the beginning of my essay, and indicated how I have done so?' This is a good reason for beginning your essay by formulating a question as specifically as possible (Unit 3). Your essay is a fair (but not necessarily the final) answer to that question.

Another characteristic of completeness is when your essay makes sense in sequence and reads as an apparently complete journey through the material. Ask yourself whether the essay can be read through, step-by-step, from beginning to end. The process of forcing yourself to read your work all the way through will give you a reasonable sense of whether you are nearly there. Something to guard against is the sense that your essay is an extension of yourself (and hence that you are yourself subject to some kind of 'final judgement'). Given the personal nature of much work in literary studies, this is a particular danger. But the reality is rather different. Finishing is in part a process of shedding something: once submitted, the essay is no longer you but a separate object. In this respect, it can be an interesting experience to read over something you have written some time previously; the alien feeling your essay will probably create can be very strong, making it completely clear that it was never really *you* but something you produced at a particular time which may now seem barely recognisable as your own.

Remember, too, that the problem of completion is one reason why your assessors have set a word limit and a time limit (deadline); these contrived limits force you to rank tasks in terms of relative priority, and give you a straightforward, practical way of deciding whether lower priority tasks are achievable within the given boundaries.

BIBLIOGRAPHY

When you write an essay you refer to other books, chapters and articles (and perhaps to other kinds of text, in other media). The list of these texts is sometimes called your **documentation**, and is usually given at the end of the essay as your bibliography. A bibliography should normally contain all and only the texts that you cite in the course of your essay, so that every entry in the bibliography matches a citation. If you wish to add texts that you read but did not actually cite, put them in a separate list. Alternatively, if it seems appropriate, manufacture a citation for them along the lines of 'for further discussion of X, see . . .'.

The principles underlying a bibliography are these.

1. For each item, include enough information to enable a reader to find that item. (This has to be at a rather general level, so that a reader who is not in your physical environment can still use it, so for example do not include a book's catalogue number that only applies in one particular library.)

2. Follow prescribed rules for what information you should include, and in what order it should be given; and be consistent in using these rules.

3. Ensure that each in-text citation matches an entry in the bibliography, and that it is always possible to pair them up. If there are two authors with the same last name, differentiate the in-text citations with initials; if there are two texts with the same author and both were published in 1995, differentiate the in-text citation as 1995a and 1995b (see also Unit 13).

4. Ensure that the bibliography is ordered: alphabetically by author's last name, and for each author ordered by the date of each text.

5. Bibliographies can be divided into sections, each with its own alphabetical ordering where appropriate: e.g. by media, by primary vs secondary sources.

Principle 2 above usually overrides principle 1, by telling you exactly what to include. But principle 1 can be useful for unusual kinds of source (e.g. non-printed sources) in cases where the prescribed rules give no advice.

As a general guide, the following types of information about a document should be included in your bibliography.

1. The first (leftmost) thing in a bibliographic entry is the author's name. Usually the last name comes first, followed by first name or initials (so that the bibliography can be sequenced by last name). Sometimes, if there are several authors, the first author has last-first name order and the other authors have first-last name order. If the document you are citing is an edited book, the name or names are followed by 'ed' or 'eds'. If there is no author's name, usually you start your entry with the title of the book; you can, if needed, also use 'Anon'.

2. Date of publication. If you don't know the date, write 'no date' (or n.d.). If you are looking in a book for its date of publication, remember that it could be either at the beginning or the end. Give the date of the edition you are actually using (not, for example, the date of first publication); if you think it is relevant to give the date of original publication, put it in some clearly marked way, such as square brackets and say 'first published'.

3. Title of the document. Book titles are differentiated from article or chapter titles in various ways depending on the referencing system. Usually book titles are indicated either by underlining or italicising them. As a further differentiation, single quotes are commonly used round chapter or article titles.

4. Place of publication, followed by name of publisher.

5. If your document is contained in another document – for example, if it is an article in a journal or a chapter in a book – you must include information about that other document (usually italicised or underlined), and the page numbers for the article or chapter in question. If the containing document is a book, you will need to give its authors or editors; if it is a journal, all you need is the journal title.

Your teachers will probably give you specific rules to decide whether date comes before or after title, whether you need initials or full first name, etc. If you are not given specific rules, we suggest the following (where 'full stop' is the period symbol).

In general:

last name , initial . date . title . place of publication : publisher

Where there are two or more authors, add them as '*and initial . last name*'; add (ed.) or (eds) for editors. Italicise the title of a book or journal; leave other titles unitalicised (and do not surround them with quotes).

Where you have a document inside a document, after *title* instead of *place of publication: publisher* add this:

- for an edited book:

    In + [all the 'general' information for the book as above] + page numbers

- for a journal:

    Journal title italicised + . + volume number : page numbers

Here are some examples which follow this pattern.

- Book

    > Briggs, K.M. 1970. *A Dictionary of British Folk Tales in the English Language*. London: Routledge.

- Chapter in book

    > Hayes, B. 1989. The Prosodic Hierarchy in Meter. In Kiparsky, P. and G. Youmans (eds) 1989. *Phonetics and Phonology 1: Rhythm and meter*. San Diego: Academic Press. pp. 201–260.

- Article in journal (here, the journal *Language* volume 72).

    > Hanson, K. and P. Kiparsky 1996. A Parametric Theory of Poetic Meter. *Language*. 72: 287–335.

Bibliographic software

It is possible to buy software to help you organise your bibliography. The main advantage is that you can gather a large bibliography as you work, which you can then draw on for specific purposes such as an article. Such software can be useful, but may not be preferable

– especially if you are writing coursework essays rather than publishing research – to the simpler alternative of just keeping a single large Microsoft® Word (or similar) file containing entries for all the works you have used.

FOOTNOTES AND ENDNOTES

Some citation systems use footnotes (the 'notes' or 'notes and bibliography' systems). In general, we suggest that you avoid using footnotes or endnotes for anything other than citation. If you want to say something which is important for your argument, you should put it into the prose of your essay, not hang it off the bottom or at the end. If the point you wish to make is not well integrated into your argument, then you should consider not saying it at all. Remember that your reader may not read your footnotes; hence you may, in effect, be throwing material away by putting it there.

ABSTRACT OR SUMMARY

An **abstract** is a short (usually 100–200 word) summary of your essay, but is usually only required for longer coursework projects or dissertations. The abstract guides your reader to an understanding of the essay's key points. As the first thing your marker reads in cases where one is required, your abstract can also function as an advertisement, to draw the reader in and give a positive first impression of your essay; a good abstract will already start to influence how your work is likely to be marked. The abstract might have the following component parts:

• the question or questions you are asking,
• the main answers to those questions,
• the texts you are using,
• the theories or methods you are using.

Writing an abstract will help you think about your writing from a new point of view, forcing you to assess for yourself what is interesting about it.

TABLE OF CONTENTS

If your essay or dissertation has named sections and sub-sections, it can be a good idea to add a **table of contents** at the beginning. The first purpose of such a table of contents is to tell the reader exactly what she will find in your essay, and which page to find it on. But there is also a second purpose. Like an abstract, a table of contents requires you to look at and decide what is in your essay, to outline its development once more. As we have said in Unit 7, you should be able to read your own table of contents (or abstract, or outline) and get a sense of what the essay says. If titles of sections are vague or uninformative (or boring, vague or cliched), it may be that these sections lack focus and purpose. If even you can't see any clear development through the essay when you look at your own table of contents, this may be because the essay has failed to achieve any clear development and is not yet finished. Remember that you can create and format a table of contents (TOC) automatically if you are word-processing your essay, and can update it automatically. You can then link this process to using 'outline view' in Microsoft® Word or similar programs in order to make the logic of your argument clearer by moving sections around (see Unit 7). After using such tools, however, remember to read through the main body of your text once more to adjust local sign-posting, which is the glue between the essay's different elements or sections.

ACKNOWLEDGEMENTS

The **acknowledgements** at the beginning of a published work or dissertation – generally not in coursework essays and never in exams – allow you to thank people and organisations. If you have been given permission to reproduce material, you will usually have to thank the authors or publishers who have given that permission. You may have had useful discussions with particular people, or used their ideas; these people's names might be included. You may wish to emphasise, following convention, that you take complete responsibility for the way ideas are represented, even if they aren't your own, so that any mistakes or adverse judgement will not be directed towards the people you have named.

There are also forms of institutional help that might be acknowledged, including technical help (e.g. typing) or financial help (e.g. grants or scholarships). In a research dissertation you should say if any part of your thesis or essay is related to conference papers you have given or articles you have published; one side-effect of this is to show that your work has already gained some degree of acceptance and circulation.

FINAL STAGE BEFORE SUBMITTING

Before handing in your finished manuscript, here is a checklist to go through.

1. Check spelling, particularly the spelling of names. Use a word-processor's spell-checker at the almost-final stage (rather than before), overriding it and supplementing it where necessary. Remember that the spell-checker may not catch when you have used the wrong word (e.g. 'were' instead of 'where').

2. Check grammatical errors, such as lack of agreement between subject and verb. Computer software sometimes includes a grammar checker, which as a student of English you will probably find more convenient to disable, so as not to be harassed by its suggestions.

3. If you have compiled your table of contents manually, add the final page numbers.

4. If you use a documentation system that separates the citation from a full bibliographic entry at the end, make sure that all citations match bibliographic entries. (Since your citations always include dates, a shortcut way of doing this is to search your text for four-digit numbers.)

5. Check the bibliography for completeness and consistency.

6. Check through the text for incomplete parts. When you are writing, it can be helpful to use a consistent symbol, such as a

percentage sign or other infrequently used character, to indicate something that needs to be followed up later (or, as we have said, consider using colour for such material). As a final procedure, it is then possible to search through the text for any remaining percentage signs, and deal with them.

7. Once you have made all the photocopies you need, check that they all have all the pages, that they are numbered continuously, and that they are in the right order.

8. Make sure you have complied with regulations for submission (this is best done before you even start, but better late than never); those regulations may include requirements about whether the essay must be typed, whether the paper has to be a particular size or of a particular kind, what margins you should leave, etc. Many of these aspects of the overall layout of the document can be added automatically at the end with many software programmes. As a general guideline, we suggest using as much space as possible in the final submission: double-spaced lines, with large margins; starting new pages where possible; and avoiding unusual fonts and colour.

PREPARING FOR A VIVA

The full name for what is usually just called a 'viva' is **viva voce**, which means 'by or with the living voice' and is the name for an oral examination on written work. Postgraduate students, who are assessed on the basis of a dissertation or thesis, usually get examined at least in part by viva; undergraduates (in our experience) rarely do unless there is a specific issue to be investigated, such as questionable authenticity of the work or plagiarism.

Functions of a viva

• The viva can test that the work is your own, by finding out whether you know what is in the dissertation or thesis, and whether you know what the author of such a study ought to know if they really wrote it themselves.

- The viva can help examiners decide on which side of a borderline you fall, including whether you pass or fail.
- The viva can function as a means of evaluating your oral skills, including your ability to improvise and argue on the spot. This function often gives a viva a 'ritual' or 'spectacle' mode, particularly in academic cultures where it is a public event.
- The viva is an event you can use to explore the possibility of publishing the thesis or part of it, particularly in discussion with an examiner who is from outside your own institution (an external examiner).

How to prepare for a viva

- Read what you have written. Pick out the key claims and be prepared to develop or promote them further. Pick out weak parts and be prepared to defend them (or to concede defeat on them if necessary). You may also need to justify any attacks you have made on particular critics or theories, so you should identify the polemical aspects of your work in advance and decide what to say about them.
- Predict those passages in the work that you will want to cite; put in bookmarks so you can find them easily.
- Ask someone – your supervisor perhaps – to do a mock viva with you. Ask them to simulate fairly, but in general to be tough and present you with genuinely challenging counter-arguments.
- Be able to summarise your dissertation or thesis in terms that can be understood by a non-specialist.
- Be ready to explain in a few sentences why your work is interesting, and prepare for the question: 'what was the most important discovery you made?'
- Think of implications of your work, including further questions, parallel cases or practical applications that you do not discuss but which are implied in your findings.
- Finally, remember that many dissertations and theses are failed or referred back for further work because they contain too many typographical errors. Before the viva try to find errors and

prepare replacement pages in order to speed up the process of re-submission and final acceptance.

PUBLISHING YOUR WORK

If you are a postgraduate, you should try to publish your thesis, or part of it. You will, however, face some typical problems. First, the manuscript you have written may be too long and may need to be shortened. A journal article is not likely to be longer than 60 double-spaced pages, and a book not longer than 70–80,000 words. Second, although most regulations for postgraduate theses say that the work must be in whole or in part 'of publishable quality', the gap between this and actually getting work published can still be considerable. One common problem is that the work as you have written it is not sufficiently contextualised for any given journal in which you wish to publish it; articles need to be shaped for a particular journal, referring to specific bodies of theoretical or critical work. It is also important to remember that by sending your work to a journal or publisher you are making a professional commit-ment which includes all the commitments you made as a student, particularly the commitment not to have plagiarised other people's work.

If you wish to publish an article, it is often best to send an abstract first along with an enquiry to the journal's editor; and it helps if you have looked at the journal and know something about their accept-ance policy and the kind of articles they publish. Most journals will reject even good articles immediately if they do not fit with their policy on kinds of content. If you hope to publish your thesis as a book, ask someone for help or advice – such as your viva examiners. Remember that it is always possible to 'self-publish' by putting your work on your own website; but before doing so you should note that some journals consider this to be prior publication and will not accept the piece of work as a submission.

EXERCISES

1. Write an abstract for a short essay that you have already written. Keep the abstract to 50 words or less.

2. Here is a bibliography which needs some work. Correct it as well as you can, and make a note of anything that will need to be looked up or checked again.

Hynes S. 'Moral Models' (1976), in Page's William Golding: Novels 1954–67.
Kinkead-Weekes M. and Gregor. *William Golding, A Critical Study*. Faber and Faber: London (1967).
Page N. (Ed.) 1985 *William Golding: Novels* (in the Casebook Series). macmillan education Ltd.,
Peter J. 1957 *The Fables of William Golding*, in Page's William Golding: Novels, 1954–67
Tiger V. (1974). *William Golding, the Dark Fields of Discovery*.

Bibliography

Note: A large number of reference works are referred to in Unit 6 to illustrate the many different kinds of information resource that are available. The latest editions of those works should be used where possible, and will be easy to locate by title in libraries and bookshops; they are not listed again here. Some style guides (e.g. *MHRA Style Guide*) can be downloaded from the relevant internet site, so it is always worth checking this alternative source of documentation. Dictionaries, encyclopedias, glossaries, guides and handbooks besides those listed in Unit 6 should be consulted as available; in many cases, such works can be consulted online as well as in printed versions. Before using unfamiliar works, however, check for suitability against the criteria for secondary sources outlined in Unit 6. Books listed below either provide fuller description of core topics, or suggest ways of extending your work in areas where space has inevitably limited our discussion.

Barnet, S. and W. Cain. 2003. *A Short Guide to Writing about Literature*. 9th edition. New York: Longman.
(relatively traditional introductory account of processes involved in writing essays in literary studies; practical and well supported by examples)

Bell, M. 2004. *Understanding English Spelling*. Cambridge: Pegasus Educational.
(accessible guide to regularities and also irregularities in English spelling)

Butcher, J. 1992. *Copy-editing: the Cambridge handbook for editors, authors and publishers.* 3rd edition. Cambridge: Cambridge University Press.
(far more detailed than you will need, but comprehensive and authoritative guide to editing for publication and other kinds of formal presentation)

Cameron, D. 1995. *Verbal Hygiene.* London: Routledge.
(historical and critical account of how people have tried to prescribe language use, including restricting or even prohibiting some types of language being used)

Carter, R., A. Goddard, D. Reah, K. Sanger and M. Bowring. 2001. *Working with Texts: A core introduction to language analysis.* 2nd edition. London: Routledge.
(wide-ranging practical workbook; numerous activities linked by commentary)

Crystal, D. (ed.). 2003. *The Cambridge Encyclopedia of the English Language.* 2nd edition. Cambridge: Cambridge University Press.
(one-stop overview of the English language; useful not only as reference resource but also for browsing)

Kirkham, S. 1989. *How to Find Information in the Humanities.* London: Library Association.
(detailed guide to learning resources that are likely to be useful for literary and related projects)

Lodge, D. 1992. *The Art of Fiction: Illustrated from classic and modern texts.* Harmondsworth: Penguin.
(short chapters each working outwards from discussion of a given example into more general techniques for analysing narrative writing)

Lynn, S. 2005. *Texts and Contexts: Writing about literature with critical theory.* 4th edition. New York: Longman.
(widely used in U.S. freshman composition courses that introduce literature; attempts to integrate contemporary critical theory into practice-based approach to essay-writing)

Marsh, N. 2001. *How to Begin Studying English Literature.* Basingstoke: Palgrave.

(basic guide to traditional approaches to studying literature; probably more useful at school level than in higher education)

Modern Humanities Research Association. 2002. *MHRA Style Guide: a handbook for authors, editors, and writers of theses.* London: Modern Humanities Research Association.

(style guide prescribed by some journals and universities; definitive statement of the 'notes and bibliography' alternative to 'author-date' systems)

Miller, C. and K. Swift. 1995. *The Handbook of Non-sexist Writing for Writers, Editors and Speakers.* 3rd edition, updated and edited by K. Mosse. London: Women's Press.

(critical discussion and detailed recommendations regarding how to avoid biased and inappropriately gender-marked writing)

Montgomery, M., A. Durant, N. Fabb, T. Furniss and S. Mills. 2000. *Ways of Reading: Advanced reading skills for students of English literature.* 2nd edition. London: Routledge.

(short chapters with exercises teaching skills of close reading and analysis for literature courses, focusing especially on literary uses of language)

Peck, J. and M. Coyle. 1999. *The Student's Guide to Writing: Grammar, punctuation and spelling.* Basingstoke: Macmillan.

(introductory guide to avoiding common pitfalls of academic writing)

University of Chicago Press. 2003. *The Chicago Manual of Style.* 15th edition. London and Chicago: University of Chicago Press.

(intended for U.S. professional academics and postgraduate students; almost 1000 pages of advice on how to format your work)

Williams, R. 1983. *Keywords: A vocabulary of culture and society.*
Revised and expanded edition. London: Fontana.
   (dictionary-style discussion of the history and shifting meanings
   of important terms used in conflicting senses in cultural and
   political discourse)

Index